Psychology: The Hope of a Science

Gregory A. Kimble

A Bradford Book
The MIT Press
Cambridge, Massachusetts
London, England

This book was set in Palatino by Graphic Composition, Inc. and was printed and bound in the United States of America.

Library of Congress Cataloging-in-Publication Data

Kimble, Gregory A.
  Psychology: the hope of a science / Gregory A. Kimble.—1st ed.
    p.   cm.
  "A Bradford book"
  Includes bibliographical references and index.
  ISBN 0–262–11204–3 (alk. paper)
  1. Psychology.   I. Title.
BF121.K53   1996
150'.1—dc20   95–21458
                                                                   CIP

For Lucille, who put up with me through all of this

Contents

Preface

When I came to psychology over fifty years ago, the field appeared to be moving toward coherence. There was general agreement that psychology is a natural science (Kimble 1953), and the accepted doctrine of the unity of science promised unity for psychology. The big remaining question was about the shape a unified psychology would take: Would it be physiological, behavioristic, field theoretic, or something else? None of those complete psychologies ever materialized, however. Psychologists went their diverse ways, and now the discipline is so splintered that specialists in separate areas of psychology cannot communicate with one another. And some of psychology's most thoughtful scholars (Koch 1993) believe that a single science of psychology is impossible.

This book revives the hope of unity and suggests the form that psychology might have if that dream were to come true. It portrays psychology as a natural science and offers a set of axioms, fashioned after Newton's laws of motion, as the fundamental principles that hold the field together.

The argument begins with a reminder that a science of psychology must obey the rules of science: it must be deterministic, empirical, and analytic. To honor those criteria, it must be some form of behaviorism, based on stimuli and responses, because the sciences are about observable reality.

Some people in psychology react negatively to this thesis. Say "behaviorism" to a psychologist in a word association test, and the responses that you get from some of them will be words like "mindless," "heartless," "atomistic," "reductionistic," "mechanistic," "trivial," and "amoral." Exploring this attitude in depth, you will discover that these psychologists regard behaviorism as laboratory bound, committed to the concept of nomothetic lawfulness, opposed to clinical practice, and incapable of dealing with the warmth, richness, and resourcefulness of human lives (see the table on p. xi).

Although in actuality that evaluation is erroneous, a small survey of my colleagues revealed that most psychologists subscribe to some of it, and some of them subscribe to most of it. The data in the table are from twenty-four faculty and graduate students in psychology at Duke University and twelve members of the Council of Representatives of the American Psychological Association (including two of its past presidents), who indicated their acceptance or rejection of the descriptions of behaviorism presented there. The table shows the number of respondents who endorsed the item and the number of participants who endorsed different numbers of these statements. The mean is 3.06. A major purpose of this book is to correct such misunderstandings. If psychology will recognize the simple truth that it must be behavioristic—reducible to stimulus-response relationships—different areas of the discipline can be as biological, cognitive, holistic, or even humanistic as they choose.

The version of behaviorism presented here might be called *functional behaviorism*. It endorses these assumptions:

1. The behavior of organisms is the product of evolution; the most basic laws of psychology apply across a range of species.
2. Because the evolution of behavior is organic evolution, the laws of psychology must be compatible with the facts of biology.
3. Human conduct evolved in response to the demands of the physical environment. All behavior—even behavior that brings misery to people—aims at adaptation to that environment.

The following statements introduce my candidates for the status of Newtonian principles of psychology:

1. Behavior is the joint product of relatively enduring *potentials* for and relatively temporary *instigations* to action. *Potentials* are the abiding characteristics of organisms; *instigations* are more transient circumstances that activate potentials or suppress them.
2. Behavior is a blend of just two ways of dealing with the environment: *adapting* to events that organisms cannot control and *coping* when control is possible.
3. Behavior happens when the strength of a potential exceeds a *threshold*.
4. Behavior is under the simultaneous control of the opponent processes of *excitation* and *inhibition*.
5. The master plan that guides behavior is *hierarchical organization*.

A major subplot in this story comes from Aristotle. These principles operate in a three-dimensional domain, of which the axes are knowing (cognition), feeling (affect), and doing (reaction tendencies).

A Caricature of Behaviorism

Description	Number of respondents endorsing item
1. Behaviorism sacrifices mind, purpose, thought, and human experience at the altar of stimuli and responses. It rejects everything that is mentalistic, thus everything that psychology is supposed to be about.	13
2. Behaviorism's stimulus-response approach is atomistic. By its very nature, behaviorism cannot deal with complete individuals or total situations.	15
3. Behavioristic explanations are reductionistic: human behavior is either materialistic biology or abstract mathematical equations.	16
4. The laws that behaviorism seeks are mechanistic laws of passive adaptation. There is no place for human beings conceived as self-directed coping, causal agents.	16
5. The behavioristic approach is nomophetic. It deals with averages and promotes the concept of "standard man." It neglects the variance in behavior and fails to recognize that every human being is a unique individual.	10
6. Behaviorism is "scientistic" not scientific. It presumes to measure human attributes that are not quantitative. Its laboratory methods are artificial. They dissect behavior from its natural context and yield results that have no useful application.	5
7. Behaviorism is simplistic. It lacks the complexity required to capture the subtle nuances and the richness of its subject matter.	15
8. Behaviorism's contributions to the understanding of the human condition are trivial. They are a catalog of small effects produced by insignificant causes.	2
9. Behaviorism turns human beings into lower animals. It is insensitive to the scope of human potential and blind to the essential human quality in all of us.	11
10. Behaviorism is without human values, without a conscience, without morality or ethics.	12

Frequency Distribution of Items Endorsed

Frequency	9	5	6	1	3	3	5	1	2	0	1
Items endorsed	0	1	2	3	4	5	6	7	8	9	10

It has taken me most of the last decade to conclude that these principles are basic and that my summary statements are the best way to present them. Toward the end of that period, I had occasion (Kimble 1990a) to review James's *Principles of Psychology*. In the process, I discovered that the book contained all my orienting evolutionary assumptions and axioms of action. In this book, I present those ideas in contexts that are diverse enough to suggest that if James had foreseen things to come, he might have elected them to be his principles of psychology.

Much has happened to psychology in the century since James; to me, the new developments, even the parallel distributed processing (PDP) models of cognition, seem to fit the scheme I have described. In their summary description of such models, David Rumelhart and his colleagues (1986) present conceptions that appear to be close kin to my five principles: (1) States of activation and net input play, respectively, the roles of potential and of instigation. (2) Associative learning and regularity discovery (of "interesting" patterns in the environment) are like mechanisms that underlie adaptation and coping. The PDP models include the concepts of (3) threshold and (4) excitation and inhibition quite explicitly. (5) Connectivity matrices are forms of hierarchical organization.

In the burgeoning field of psychopathology, (1) vulnerability and risk are potentials; disordered personalities are instigated expressions of those potentials. (2) Obsessions and compulsions are maladaptive forms of adaptation and coping. (3) The diasthesis-stress interpretation of psychopathology is a threshold model. (4) Neurotic conflict—aggression and sexuality versus anxiety and conformity—is between varieties of excitation and inhibition; when inhibition wins the battle, the conflict is repressed. (5) The structure of personality is a hierarchical organization.

If I were beginning my own *Principles of General Psychology* (1956) today, it might become two volumes, spelling out the implications of these generalities for the entire subject matter of our field. Instead, I have provided a broad outline and filled in enough of the details to encourage the science of psychology to complete the picture of my hope for the future of psychology, not only as a science but also as a means of promoting human welfare.

Acknowledgments

Although the shortcomings of this book are my responsibility, there are fewer of them than there might have been because of the help I received from many colleagues. Elise Axelrod, Herbert Crovitz, Robert Erickson, Lynn Hasher, Gregory Lockhead, Nestor Schmajuk, John Staddon, Lise Wallach, and Michael Wallach, here at Duke, and Fred McManus of Hyde Park, New York, read some or all of early drafts of the manuscript and offered criticism that made me rethink many of my arguments and improve my ways of expressing them. I thank Ernest R. Hilgard, Nicholas Wade, and one reviewer who remained anonymous, who read a nearly final version of the manuscript and made constructive comments.

The people at The MIT Press were also very helpful. I appreciate in particular Amy Pierce's support of this project, which is surely not her favorite flavor of psychology. Bev Miller made substantial improvements to the clarity of my presentation, and Sandra Minkkinen was always resourceful when dealing with my requests throughout the process of production. Finally, I owe a special debt to my coauthors of several previous publications. What I say about psychopathology, biological and physiological psychology, perception, behavioral genetics, and psychological development—and the words I use to say it—are better than they otherwise would be because of what I learned from Norman Garmezy, Kurt Schlesinger, John Werner, and Edward Zigler.

Chapter 1

Psychology as a Natural Science

When William James (1842–1910) looked at psychology a century ago, what he saw was unattractive: "A string of raw facts; a little gossip and wrangle about opinions; a little classification and generalization on the mere descriptive level; a strong prejudice that we *have* states of mind, but not a single law in the sense that physics shows us laws, not a single proposition from which any consequence causally can be deduced. We don't even know the terms between which the elementary laws would obtain if we had them. . . . This is no science, it is only the hope of a science" (James 1893, p. 468).

This book grew out of the belief that, today, that hope is brighter; that there are general principles of behavior that apply throughout the discipline, from the firings of a single neuron to the misfirings of a mind in madness.

Hallmarks of the Scientific Method

The development of the case for a unified psychology begins with a review of three "isms," the assumptions that bring the sciences together and distinguish them from other ways of interpreting natural phenomena: empiricism, elementism, and determinism. The principle of empiricism requires the knowledge of psychology to be based on observation rather than authority or intuition. The principle of elementism requires psychology to reduce phenomena to components, instead of accepting them at face value as unanalyzable wholes. The principle of determinism requires a treatment of behavior and experience as events with natural causes, instead of manifestations of God's purposes or individual free will.

James understood these criteria and although he disliked their implications, he accepted them for science. On empiricism, James said that "'scientific' conceptions must prove their worth by being 'verified'" (James 1890a, 1:v); on analysis, that *"brain and mind alike consist of simple elements"* (1:29); on determinism, that he saw no reason why *"for scientific purposes* one need give it up. [In the face of] indeterminism, science simply *stops"* (2:576).

Empiricism
Nothing forces psychology to be a science; there are other ways to understand behavior. Poets, preachers, philosophers, and people on the street also have their ways of knowing, but their criteria of truth are different. Science is empirical. For the scientist, truth is in the public facts of observation. For the poet, truth resides in personal insight and intuition. The acceptance of those subjective data as the ingredients of science mistakes private truth for public truth. In psychology, it spawns an epistemological elitist class, like Titchener's trained introspectionists, whose experiences are the only ones that are legitimate. For the preacher, truth is in the sacred texts and language of the church. The promotion of those truths replaces observation with authority, sometimes with malignant consequences, like the Scopes Monkey Trial and the Spanish Inquisition. For the philosopher, truth comes from the exercise of reason; the outside world, if it exists, is of secondary interest. For ordinary people, truth is what they have learned from personal experience—what everybody knows, what only stands to reason, and what is obviously true because the language says it is. In large measure, psychology's struggle to earn the credentials of a science has been a history of avoiding these other roads to truth.

British Empiricism   The conception of psychology as an empirical science originated in the efforts of philosophers to answer fundamental questions: How do people come to know the world? What are the origins of mind? Is knowledge inborn, or is it learned? Over a period of some two hundred years, a group of British thinkers developed the argument for learning. In *An Essay Concerning Human Understanding* (1690), John Locke (1637–1704), borrowing a metaphor from Aristotle, put this position in emphatic terms: "Let us then suppose the Mind to be, as we say, white paper [*tabula rasa*], void of all character, without any ideas. How comes it to be furnished? . . . To this I answer, in one word, from EXPERIENCE." Locke's statement was a vigorous expression of one meaning of the term "empiricism": the idea that who and what a person is depends on experience.

Public Observability   Generalized to science, empiricism took on a second meaning. It became an axiom of method: the proposition that knowledge of the world, including knowledge of the minds of other people, is suitable for science only when it is based on public observation. Reflection will reveal that, for psychology, the only public facts available are the things that organisms do and the situations in which they do them—responses and stimuli. The science of psychology must be a behavioristic stimulus-response psychology, fashioned out of those materials.

Surprisingly, perhaps, William James was one of those who understood this point. Although he defined psychology as "the Science of Mental Life, both of its phenomena and their conditions" (James 1890a, 1:1), he also noted that the fact that mental phenomena "lead to *acts* is of course the most familiar of truths" (1:5) and that "my thinking is first last and always for the sake of my doing" (2:333).

Elementism: Analysis and Synthesis
The second trademark of the scientific method is analysis, of which the most elegant versions are quantitative. Natural events are so complicated that even talking about them requires that observations be reduced to categories, and measurement facilitates communication.

The Psychologist's Fallacy   This criterion is not universally popular. William James, among others, disliked it. He was offended by "the array of younger experimental psychologists, bent on studying the *elements* of mental life, dissecting them out from the results in which they are embedded, and as far as possible reducing them to quantitative scales" (James 1890a, 1:192). But James, writing in another mood, also noted that the insistence that psychological interpretations mimic common sense is the psychologist's fallacy: "the confusion of a phenomenon of interest with the psychologist's own standpoint" (1:196). And he understood the necessity for analysis: "The less we analyze a thing, and the fewer of its relations we perceive, the less we know about it and the more our familiarity with it is of the acquaintance-type" (1:221).

The Aristotelian Elements   The earliest of British empiricism held that the elements of mind are primitive sensations, produced by sensory stimulation. Sensations, in their turn, give rise to elementary images or ideas. Later, scholars in the same tradition added elementary emotions, such as pleasure, pain, and anger, and elements of "conation" (striving), such as habit and volition. These categories correspond to the human faculties identified by Aristotle (384–322 BC) as knowing ("mind"), feeling ("appetite"), and doing ("motion").

Knowing and feeling are what contemporary psychology calls, respectively, *cognition* and *affect*. Cognition is the art and practice of understanding; it encompasses such mental processes as thinking, reasoning, and problem solving. Affect is the experience associated with motivation and emotion; it includes such states as arousal, tension, energy, and excitement. The third constituent has no generally accepted name—"conation," which some of the British empiricists suggested, has too much affect in it—but *reaction tendency* has the needed connotations. It refers to such inclinations as habit, mental set, response biases, and skill. The discussions in this book will find these categories useful in a variety of contexts.

The Pyramid of Sciences   Every science has its elements, but those of one science may be the wholes of another. The experiences and actions that psychology treats as units are constructed out of simpler perceptions, urges, and responses. These psychological primitives are the wholes of neuroscience, which seeks to understand them in terms of its own physiological and biochemical elements. Moving in the other direction, the behavior of individuals, the wholes of psychology, are the elements of political science and sociology. The key question is not so much about the integrity of wholes as it is about the processes of synthesis that organize the elements of a science to create these wholes.

Synthesis   The analysis of psychic phenomena into elements leads to a question: What is the rule of synthesis that brings the elements together to create experience as we know it? The answer of the empiricistic philosophers was that the process is *association*. The mind organizes its ideas by forming "mental strings" that tie the elements together.

Determinism

The human view of things has always been self-centered. People think of the earth as the center of the universe. They see themselves as the best of God's inventions: divine creations endowed with talents not possessed by other animals—a true language, the ability to reason, an understanding of their own mortality, and free will. Three successive revolutions in the history of ideas demolished these presumptions.

The Copernican Revolution   The first conceit to capitulate to science was the conception of the earth as the center of the universe. By the end of the second century A.D., Ptolemy, the great Greek-Egyptian geographer and astronomer, had developed the earth-centered view in ways that handled what was known about the solar system very well. And for more than a millennium, the human ego remained safely situated in a pivotal position in the cosmic scheme of things. Early in the fifteenth century, however, Nicholas Copernicus (1473–1573) proved that the sun rather than the earth is at the center of the solar system. This insight meant that what had been the hub of everything was nothing but a fly speck floating in the heavens.

The Darwinian Revolution   The second blow to human superiority was delivered by Sir Charles Darwin (1809–1882), whose theory maintained that homo sapiens evolved from lower forms of life and has no claim to being a unique creation. Darwin offered data to suggest that lower creatures have human-like emotions and the elements of intellect. Might they not, then, also have the beginnings of a language, some appreciation of their own mortality, and the rudiments of free will?

Victorian morality reacted negatively to Darwinism. As one Philadelphia mainline matron is reported to have said, "Evolution? Descended from apes? My dear, we will hope that it is not true. But if it is let us pray that it may not become generally known." This critical evaluation found official expression in the form of legal sanctions: laws that made it a felony to teach the theory of evolution. Eventually, of course, the evidence prevailed, and now Darwin's view has a status that is more like fact than theory. But the older prejudices are not entirely dead. In some states in the United States, there are "equal-time" regulations that require teachers of biology to cover biblical creationism if they present the theory of evolution.

The Psychological Revolution   Common sense attaches great significance to a distinction between the mind and body. According to this view, the actions of the body are determined by external forces, including those imposed on it by the mind. The mind, however, is self-determined. It knows the circumstances of the body and, through its own free will, dictates the body's actions. This freedom endows the behavior of human creatures, and possibly no others, with dignity and worth.

This final citadel of faith in human preeminence came under fire from a succession of psychologists, who maintained that both consciousness and free will are illusions; the operations of the mind and human conduct are just as much determined by external forces as are the functions of the body. Freud's theory of psychoanalysis was in this tradition. Freud proposed that human behavior is determined, often by unconscious forces, and that the quality of adult adjustment is the result of infantile experience, particularly sexual experience. The shock value of the sexuality in Freud's theory brought wide attention to psychoanalysis, and its influence on Western culture has been enormous. Its importance to psychology, however, is destined to be less than that of behaviorism. Too many of Freud's ideas have failed the tests of science.

Beginning with John B. Watson (1878–1958), the behaviorists have been psychology's staunchest advocates of determinism. Its important recent champion was Burrhus Frederick Skinner (1904–1990), whose first major contribution was a series of experiments, showing how conditions of reinforcement affect bar pressing in laboratory rats and key pecking in pigeons. Later, he applied the principle of reinforcement to human behavior. His novel, *Walden Two* (1948), describes the utopia he believed could be created in a society governed by the laws of reinforcement. His 1957 book, *Verbal Behavior,* applies the argument to language. Skinner's most provocative opinions appear in *Beyond Freedom and Dignity* (1971), where he makes a case against free will, insisting that people become whatever brings reward and spares them punishment.

The Schools of Psychology

As psychology developed, most psychologists continued to endorse determinism, empiricism, and analysis but with different emphases that led, early in the twentieth century, to the appearance of several schools of psychology—very general theories that covered the entire discipline.

Structuralism

The earliest of these schools was structuralism, founded by Wilhelm Wundt (1832–1920), who established the first laboratory of psychology in Leipzig, Germany, in 1879, commonly taken as scientific psychology's date of birth. One of Wundt's students, Edward B. Titchener (1867–1927), brought structuralism to America. As chair of psychology at Cornell University he promoted structuralism with vigor, making it the dominant position in American psychology for many years.

Structuralism strove to understand the structure of the mind and the content of consciousness, which, following the British empiricists, it took to be composed of sensations—sights, sounds, tastes, and tickles. Some sensations, like pure red and blue, are primary; others, like orange and purple, are constructed out of combinations of these elements. The structuralists' method of investigation was introspection, in which subjects looked inward on their experience and reported on the elements they found there.

The structuralists were extravagantly analytic. They maintained that sensations can be described in terms of several "physical dimensions of consciousness" (Titchener's phrase), such as quality, intensity, duration, and extent. The color purple combines the qualities of red and blue; because of variations in intensity, different purples may be very dark, or very light, or something in between. The structuralists' dissection of the mind into elements was similar to chemists' description of the universe in terms of molecules and atoms. The obvious parallel led to the christening of structural psychology as "mental chemistry."

The structuralists believed that the makeup of consciousness is the same for everyone—that their science would reveal the mind of "standard man." This position anticipated the modern doctrine of nomothetic lawfulness—the idea that the laws of behavior apply to people generally. The science of mental tests discovered individual differences in intelligence and personality and laid the groundwork for the alternative concept of ideographic lawfulness, according to which the laws of behavior apply only to individuals.

Gestalt Psychology

Some psychologists objected to the structuralists' atomistic stance because it violates experience. We do not see an apple as so much redness, yellowness, and roundness with a stem on top; we see it as a whole apple that resists such analysis. These psychologists demanded an approach to psychology that respects the integrity of experience. The most important version of the holistic approach was Gestalt psychology, of which Max Wertheimer (1880–1943) was the founder.

"Gestalt" is a German word for shape or form; it carries the connotation of an integrated organization that makes wholes more than the sum of their constituent parts. The Gestalt psychologists made this point with the aid of experiments on perception, showing that what we see is coherent wholes rather than the elements of visual displays. The most convincing of these demonstrations came from Wertheimer's (1912) work on the phi phenomenon (apparent motion). When two stationary lights, separated by a certain distance, are turned on and off in alternation, an observer sees one light moving back and forth, not two individual lights. This demonstration supports a Gestaltisch interpretation because the elements (two lights flashing separately) cannot explain the whole (a single moving light). The phi phenomenon does not occur unless these elements are present, but an additional process of organization is critical to this perception.

Functionalism

Another group of psychologists objected to the structuralists' preoccupation with the content of the mind. These functionalists, greatly influenced by Darwin's theory of evolution, maintained that the purpose of the mind is to promote survival of the organism and that psychology should be studying these uses rather than the forms of consciousness.

One of the giants in the history of functionalism was William James, who found the basic functionalist idea in the writings of Herbert Spencer (1820–1903). James wrote, "On the whole, few recent formulas have done more real service of a rough sort in psychology than the Spencerian one that the essence of mental life and bodily life are one, namely 'the adjustment of inner to outer relations'" (James 1890a, 1:6). James also knew of Darwin's work, and he proposed that the actions of the nervous system "have usually the common character of being of service. They ward off the noxious stimulus and support the beneficial one; whilst if, in itself indifferent, the stimulus be a sign of some distant circumstance of practical importance, the animal's acts are addressed to this circumstance so as to avoid its perils or secure its benefits" (1:12). James believed that, as correlates of nervous activity, mental states had purposes. He spoke of consciousness as a fighter for ends that, but for its presence, would not be ends at all (1:141).

The functionalists accepted the structuralists' introspective method, but they were clear that introspection had problems. As James noted, the method provides direct knowledge only of the mind of the introspectionist; the knowledge of other minds is inference. "[Peter] may have a *knowledge,* and a correct one too, of what Paul's last drowsy states of mind were as he sank into sleep, but it is an entirely different sort of knowledge from that which he has of his own last states. He *remembers* his own states, whilst he only *conceives* of Paul's" (James 1890a, 1:239). And then: How can a mind even know itself? Does that not require the postulation of a little man inside the head to do the knowing? Or, perhaps, "a parliament of little men together, each of whom as happens also in a real parliament, possesses but a single idea which he ceaselessly tries to make prevail" (1:29). How can introspection grasp the dynamic aspects of experience, the "flights" between the "perchings" in the stream of thought? They are past events before the mind can catch them: "The attempt at introspective analysis in these cases is in fact like seizing a spinning top to catch its motion, or trying to turn up the gas fast enough to see how the darkness looks" (1:244).

Behaviorism
Although Watson, the father of behaviorism, criticized all the other schools, he accepted the traditional themes that they endorsed. He was a vigorous advocate of empiricism but with a difference. Recognizing the importance of public observability, Watson proposed that private mental states cannot be the subject matter of a scientific discipline precisely because they are private: "The behaviorist asks: Why don't we make what we can *observe* the real field of psychology? . . . Now what can we observe? Well we can observe *behavior—what the organism does or says*" (Watson 1925, p. 6).

There was no place in such a science for the concepts of mind or consciousness or for the introspective method: "[Consciousness is] just as unprovable, just as unapproachable, as the old concept of the soul. And to the behaviorist the two terms are essentially identical, so far as concerns their metaphysical implications. . . . This thing we call consciousness can be analyzed only by *introspection*" (Watson 1925, pp. 5–6).

Watson accepted the necessity of analysis but not the structuralists' elements. Implicitly recognizing the Aristotelian categories (of knowing, feeling, and doing), he noted that "in the analyses of consciousness made by certain of the [structural] psychologists you find such elements as *sensations* and their ghosts, the *images*. With others, you find not only sensations, but so-called *affective elements;* in still others you find such elements as *will*—the so-called conative element in consciousness" (Watson 1925, p. 5). Watson's elements were reflexes, and his principle of associationism was Pavlovian conditioning.

Watson endorsed environmental as opposed to biological determinism and stated his position forcefully: "Give me a dozen healthy infants, well formed, and my own specified world to bring them up in, and I'll guarantee to take any one at random and train him to become any kind of specialist I might select—doctor, lawyer, artist, merchant-chief, and yes, even beggar-man and thief—regardless of his talents, penchants, tendencies, abilities, vocations and race of his ancestors" (Watson 1925, p. 104).

Watson was a brilliant writer. After he left the Johns Hopkins University, driven out by a scandalous affair with a female assistant, he wrote widely for the general public, chiefly on child development. A whole generation of parents accepted Watson's teachings, thus acquiring a heavy burden of guilt because of the implication that their child-rearing practices and nothing else were responsible for their offspring's misbehavior even as adults.

Psychometric Psychology
Long before the appearance of psychology's schools, a second science of psychology, based on mental tests, was already in the making; its history goes back four thousand years. From about 2200 B.C. to A.D. 1905, the Chinese government appointed candidates to various official positions on the basis of a series of rigorous examinations, culminating in a three-day session in Beijing. The Chinese tests covered the so-called six arts: music, archery, horsemanship, writing, mathematics, and the rites and ceremonies of personal and public life. These methods of assessment were so successful that, in the nineteenth century, they became a model for personnel selection in the British and German colonial services and the U.S. civil service commission (Dahlstrom 1985). The amount of time required by these tests was so great, however, that they were abandoned when more efficient methods became available.

The modern history of the testing movement dates to 1904, when the French minister of education asked Alfred Binet (1857–1911) to find a way to identify children in the schools who were below average in ability, so that they could receive special assistance. In response to this request, Binet and his collaborator, Theophile Simon, implicitly equating the ability to do school work with intelligence, proceeded to construct a test designed to assess the talents that a child must have to succeed in school—such cognitive abilities as attention, memory, verbal and mathematical skill, and power of reasoning. Current measures of intelligence continue to emphasize this type of content.

Modern personality assessment began a few years later. In World War I, a flood of inductees into the American military created a need for methods of screening out the emotionally unfit. Responding to this need, Robert S. Woodworth (1869–1962) created a personal data sheet (1919), which produced ratings that were used to identify recruits who might not perform adequately in a military situation. Woodworth's test was the ancestor of the modern personality inventories. Just two years later, in peaceful Switzerland, the psychiatrist Hermann Rorschach (1884–1922) invented the Rorschach Inkblot Test (1921), which remains the most widely used projective method of personality assessment. It is clearer now than it was then that psychometric psychology is a different science from structuralism, behaviorism, and the rest.

Psychological Lawfulness

A science is a body of knowledge about some aspect of the world; its goal is to maximize the orderliness of that knowledge. The ingredients of order are scientific laws describing how the dependent and independent variables of a science relate to one another. *Dependent variables* are the phenomena that a science attempts to understand—in psychology, the behavior of human beings and other animals. *Independent variables* are factors that cause or predict the values of these dependent variables. The diagram,

Independent variable ——— L_1 ——— Dependent variable,

presents a general formula. L_1 refers to a Type-1 law (to distinguish it from laws of a second and a third type, to be introduced in the next chapter).

In psychology, these Type-1 laws take two different forms. The first is a set of stimulus-response (Type-S) laws, relating responses (dependent variables) to stimuli (independent variables). In this context, the term "stimulus" refers to environmental objects and events generally, not just to the atomistic elements of the structural psychologists. The term "response" refers to behavior generally, not just to the muscle twitches of the Watsonian reflexologists. Diagrammatically

Stimulus ——— Type-S law (L_1) ——— Response.

Suppose the folk saying that "practice makes perfect" is correct. It thus implies a Type-S, law which says that the quality of performance on some task increases to perfection with practice. Diagrammatically,

Practice ——— Type-S law (L_1) ——— Quality of performance,

where the L_1 law is "increases with."

The second class of Type-1 laws are Type-P, laws relating behavior to various properties (characteristics, attributes) of organisms—such things as race, sex, age, social class, physiological condition, and the psychological traits revealed by clinical interviews and mental tests. Diagrammatically,

Property of organism ——— Type-P law (L_1) ——— Response.

Every student who is in college, partly on the basis of a high SAT or ACT score, is there in recognition of the truth of such a law. This law says that, in general, the higher a student's score on these tests of scholastic aptitude is, the better is this person's school performance, measured by such indexes as grade point averages (GPA). Diagrammatically,

SAT/ACT score ——— Type-P law (L_1) ——— GPA,

where L_1, again, is "increases with."

As in this case, many Type-P laws are response-response laws, which describe the relationship between two measures of behavior, R^1 and R^2. In this example, R^1 is a student's SAT or ACT score and R^2 is that same student's GPA. It is important to recognize, however, that in addition to responses, the P in Type-P laws may refer to other properties of organisms. For example, there is evidence that an excess of the neurotransmitter dopamine may be present in the brains of schizophrenic patients and that the probability of an individual's developing that disorder increases (L_1) as a result of this condition:

Dopamine ———Type-P law (L_1)——— Probability of
level   schizophrenia,

Psychology's Two Sciences

In 1957, Lee J. Cronbach made the important observation that these two types of law differentiate two scientific disciplines that are built on psychology's two main contributions to the history of ideas: the application of the experimental method to behavior and the invention of the mental test. The first of Cronbach's two sciences is *experimental psychology,* which studies the relationships of behavior to conditions that, potentially at least, could be manipulated in the laboratory. The second is *correlational psychology,* which deals with tests and other assessments of the attributes of individuals.

Experimental psychology searches for the commonalities in behavior. It seeks to paint (the critics would say, "by the numbers") a picture of the structuralists' "standard man" that is revealed by averages and other measures of central tendency. Correlational psychology, by contrast, concentrates on the individual differences in behavior revealed by the standard deviation and other measures of dispersion. Along with William James, it sees significance in variation: "Although [experimental psychology may show that] there is very little difference between one man and another, what little there is, is very important" (James 1890b, p. 438).

The bare-bones skeletons of these two sciences, laid out in figure 1.1, reveal that they have similar ambitions: to discover the L_1 laws relating behavior to independent variables: environmental circumstances and predictors in experimental and correlational psychology, respectively. Whether a particular psychology is experimental or correlational depends on its independent variables. Sciences that go by the same name

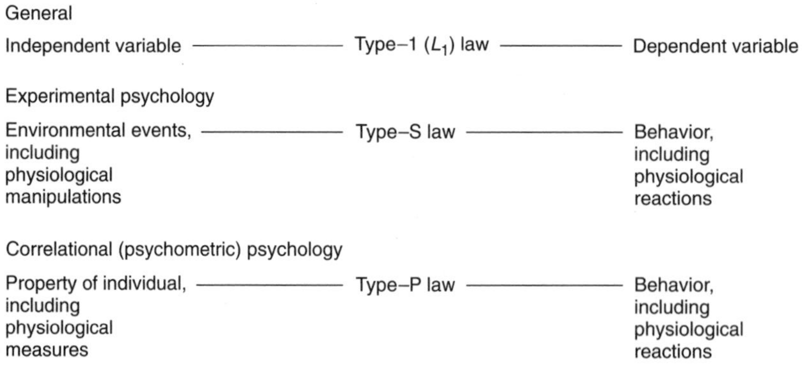

General

Independent variable ————————— Type–1 (L_1) law ————————— Dependent variable

Experimental psychology

Environmental events, ————————— Type–S law ————————— Behavior,
including   including
physiological   physiological
manipulations   reactions

Correlational (psychometric) psychology

Property of individual, ————————— Type–P law ————————— Behavior,
including   including
physiological   physiological
measures   reactions

Figure 1.1
Models of Psychology's Two Sciences
The panels summarize the relationships between independent and dependent variables in psychology. The top panel presents the general case, in which Type-1 laws connect these two classes of variables. The middle panel represents the situation of experimental psychology, in which Type-S laws link responses to events in the environments and previous experiences of individuals, including physiological manipulations. The bottom panel shows the situation of correlational psychology, in which Type-P laws relate behavior to assessments of the attributes (properties) of individuals, such as the traits measured by scores on tests, and bodily conditions, such as blood pressure and brain chemistry. The independent variables of correlational psychology can be the dependent variables of experimental psychology.

may be either. Biological psychology is correlational when physiological antecedents, like brain chemistry or brain waves, are used to predict behavior; it is experimental when these reactions are the dependent variables in experiments. Psychometric psychology is correlational when it uses scores on tests to predict behavior elsewhere; it is experimental when it investigates the impact of environmental conditions on these scores.

Correlation versus Causation

Experimental psychology is like experimental physics. Its concern is with the effects of independent variables that can be manipulated in the laboratory. Correlational psychology is like astronomy. Its independent variables cannot be manipulated. Variations in its independent variables are obtained by selecting individuals who differ in measures of these variables.

In terms of practicalities, a knowledge of the Type-S laws obtained in experimental psychology allows control as well as the prediction of behavior, whenever the scientist can manipulate the independent variables. The Type-P laws of correlational psychology permit prediction but not control because their independent variables are beyond manipulation. In some thinking, the concept of causation applies only to independent variables that are manageable. This idea appears to be the basis for the claim sometimes heard that experimental psychology is "more scientific" than correlational psychology: the laws of experimental psychology are causal laws, while those of correlational psychology are not, and, in the words of a methodological cliché, "Correlation does not prove causation."

The Concept of Causality
Statements of causality relate phenomena to something other than themselves. The cause of an event, Y, is another event, X, that has a dual relationship to Y. First, if X occurs, Y always happens (X is a sufficient cause of Y); second, if X is absent, Y never occurs (X is a necessary cause of Y). Stated in a single formula, this double definition of causality is: "If-and-only-if X, then always Y."

The X in the formula can vary. The independent variables in well-established laws provide one form of explanation. Thus, it is acceptable to say that an extra X chromosome in the twenty-first position is a cause of mental retardation in children with Down's syndrome. More tentatively (because the law is less well established), it also is legitimate to say that poverty and other environmental deprivation cause most mental retardation.

Pitfalls

Causality is a tricky concept, and it may have created more confusion than understanding for psychology. The confusions have been of two main kinds.

First, the definition of causality—"if-and-only-if X, then always Y"—implies that events have single causes. For psychological events, however, this is never true because even the simplest responses and experiences have many causes. What you see when a spot of light appears on a wall depends on the shape of the spot, several wave lengths that determine its color, the intensity of the light, the color of the wall, the stimuli that you have looked at recently, and the sensitivities of a host of mechanisms in the retina and the visual nervous system.

The medical model of psychopathology routinely fails to recognize the fact of multiple causality by making the assumption that mental disorders are single entities brought on by single causes that a patient either has or does not have. Although such diagnoses are appropriate for some medical conditions—there is only one known cause for pregnancy, and a patient is never marginally in that condition—psychological disorders are more complicated than the medical model suggests. They may be full-blown or borderline, and even "normal" people have symptoms. And, like every other important aspect of behavior, they express an array of dispositions. In terms of the Aristotelian classification, the mental disorders all involve faulty thinking, inappropriate feelings, and disordered doing. A single underlying physiological cause of such an array of symptoms seems unlikely. Moreover, the etiology of mental disorders is both environmental and biological. Even the identical twin of someone who is schizophrenic may not develop that disorder. Although the two twins have the same genotype, the environment determines its phenotypic expression.

In addition to reminding us that a science of psychology must be analytic, this complexity raises an interesting question: Do causes vary in importance? Can X be a "stronger" cause of Y than Z? The answer to this question, in a certain sense, is yes. Whether X is a more important cause than Z depends on what analysis reveals about the ingredients of Y. If Y is three-fourths A and one-fourth B, and if X causes A and Z causes B, then X is, indeed, a stronger cause of Y than Z. In the language used in answering such questions, variations in X account for more of the variation in Y than do variations in Z. Ironically, correlational psychology had this insight much earlier than experimental psychology.

The second confusion, a failure to take the "if-and-only-if X, then always Y" formula literally, leads psychology to look backward in its search for causes, whereas causality itself works forward. The formula implies research that introduces X or keeps X absent, and then notes whether Y, appropriately, is there or not. But the causes of much behavior are in the distant past, a fact that discourages such investigation. Instead, the common practice is to find two groups of individuals who display and do not display some behavioral Y (e.g., anxiety) and then look for an X (e.g., the presence of abusive parents in the family) and infer causality if that X is more common in the anxious group than in the other.

There is a classroom demonstration that illustrates two problems with such research. The teacher tells the students something like this: "Suppose, without your knowledge and just before you came to class today, someone put a drug into your drink that soon will make you behave as though you were psychotic. A few hours from now, a classmate finds you wandering on campus muttering nonsense and takes you to the student health service, whose clinicians notify the college administration and your parents of your "illness" and send you to a psychiatric hospital, where you are asked to fill out a questionnaire that inquires about events in your past life that might have caused your problem. Take some time and think about what you might write. Would you have things to report that might account for your 'psychopathological' reaction? Bring your responses (in a form that protects your identity) with you to the next class meeting."

In one such demonstration 61 Duke students in a class of about 150 (41 percent) described more than 120 incidents (some students reported more than one) that they thought might qualify:

> "I discovered that my mother had shot herself and would die unless the ambulance got there soon."
> "When I was about nine, three high school football players dragged me into the woods and began to tear my clothes off. As I was crying hysterically, one of them dropped his pants and began to have sexual activities with me. I have never gotten over these experiences and still have a phobia about wooded areas."

One problem with such retrospective research comes in two parts: (1) There are traumatic happenings in the lives of everyone that seem severe enough to bring on mental disorder; the fact that only some people succumb violates the "if-X, then *always* Y" fraction of the formula for causality. (2) Some individuals without the given X develop the disorder, thus violating the "*only-if* X, then Y" fact fraction of the formula.

Another response that I received once when I did this demonstration illustrates the second problem. One student wrote, "I was born a poor black kid but I never had any rhythm. My dog was named 'shit-head' and everyone said I was a jerk." Although it never occurred to me to question this reaction, I learned later that it is either a verbatim quote or a paraphrase of a quip by someone in the movie *The Jerk*. The problem with such data is that they are difficult to verify, even when they are honest "memories."

Summary and Conclusions

By the end of the nineteenth century, psychology had assimilated the three traditional rules that govern the operation of a science: empiricism (observation instead of intuition or authority is the source of knowledge for psychology), elementism (particles, not the wholes of everyday experience, are the components of the science), and determinism (outside forces rather than free will are the causes of behavior).

Empiricism

In order to obey the rule of empiricism, the science of psychology must be some version of stimulus-response behaviorism. Starting there, it can be biological, cognitive, or anything else it chooses. This commitment is what the diverse approaches to psychology have in common. Disciplines that study something else—like brain, mind, artificial intelligence, or human potential (without ties to stimuli and responses)—may sometimes be a science, but they are not psychology.

Analysis

The phenomena of every science are reducible to elementary units. The structuralists and behaviorists, respectively, proposed that these elements are sensations and reflexes. A different set of units that I rely on heavily in this book is traceable to Aristotle. It classifies experience and behavior into broad categories that contemporary psychology calls cognition, affect, and reaction tendencies. But elements of any kind leave something missing from the science. The functionalists took that something to be the purposes of behavior; the Gestalt psychologists missed the absence of organization. The later chapters in this book attend to those omissions.

Determinism

Over a period of several hundred years, three scientific revolutions led to the abandonment of cherished views that gave humankind a privileged position in the universe and in the animal kingdom. The first and second revolutions were launched by Copernicus and Darwin. The third involved determinism. This psychological revolution, which began with Freud and Watson and is still in progress, challenges the concept of free will and seeks explanations of behavior that involve external circumstances instead of personal dispositions.

Lawfulness

The purpose of a science is to maximize the orderliness of knowledge about some set of real-world events. In psychology, the first step toward the achievement of such order is in the development of Type-1 laws of two kinds, Type-S and Type-P that, respectively, relate behavior to stimuli and the properties of organism.

Psychology's Two Sciences

The Type-S and Type-P laws are the stock in trade of two companion sciences, experimental psychology and correlational (psychometric) psychology, both of which accept behavior as their dependent variables but differ in their independent variables. For experimental psychology, the independent variables are environmental objects and events (stimuli); for correlational psychology, they are attributes (properties) of individuals. Whether a particular psychology is one science or the other depends on its independent variables. Biological psychology is correlational when it uses physiological antecedents to predict behavior; it is experimental when these same reactions are dependent variables in experiments. Psychometric psychology is correlational when it uses test scores to predict behavior; it is experimental when it seeks the causes of these scores.

Control, Prediction, and Causality

One important consequence of the difference in their independent variables is that the laws obtained in experimental psychology make it possible, in principle, to control as well as to predict behavior. The laws obtained in correlational psychology permit prediction only. Except for that, nothing makes one of these two sciences more precise or scientific than the other. The common allegation that experimental psychology is superior because it deals with causes contains a grain of truth, but the concept of causality is elusive and, as we shall see, the difference is less important than it at first seems to be.

Chapter 2

Subjective Concepts in a World of Facts

In his behavioristic manifesto, John B. Watson promoted what has since been called radical behaviorism (Staddon 1993). He insisted that psychology must abandon mentalistic concepts, for reasons that had a certain merit: if psychology wants to be a science, it must deal with observable realities, and the only public facts available are stimuli and responses. But even psychologists who endorsed that thesis disliked the implication that Watson saw in this empiricistic truth. The argument excluding mental states from psychology, because they are private, appeared to throw out the baby (everything of interest in psychology) with the bath (subjectivity).

The Liberation of Behaviorism

There is a way to make subjective concepts legal in psychology: by treating them as inferences drawn from the public data of the science, that is, responses and the situations in which they occur. If you see someone hit or kiss another person, you cannot observe that person's hostility or love directly, but it is reasonable to interpret these acts as expressions of such private states when they take place in certain circumstances.

This insight came into psychology in two waves of understanding. First, in 1922, Edward C. Tolman offered a "new formula for behaviorism," which made the basic argument. Without using the terminology that was soon to be standard, Tolman urged psychology to treat mental states as "intervening variables" that are tied to observation by "operational definitions." For example, he defined a rat's "purpose" to obtain the food in the goal box at the end of the maze by reference to the observable quality of the animal's behavior that one might call "persistence until"—until that goal is reached (Tolman 1925). Over the years, Tolman offered operational meaning for a host of mentalistic concepts, including cognition, emotion, and consciousness (see Tolman 1951).

Second, not long after Tolman's pioneering statement, the social and behavioral sciences discovered operationism in the writings of the physicist, Percy W. Bridgman (1928), and soon such influential psychologists as Carol C. Pratt (1939), S. Smith Stevens (1939), Clark L. Hull (1943), and Kenneth W. Spence (1944), were recommending the position. The psychology that adopts this strategy is operational or methodological behaviorism (Staddon 1993). It differs from Watson's radical behaviorism in one important way: although it accepts the edict that psychology must be grounded in observation, it accepts subjective concepts, provided they are defined by reference to independent variables and related to behavior. Table 2.1 presents several examples of these intervening variables to illustrate the pattern. They will figure in the discussion throughout the remainder of this chapter.

The Intervening-Variable Approach

In several formal statements of this general idea, Tolman (e.g., 1936, 1938) replaced the Type-1 (L_1) laws described in Chapter 1 with two other sets of laws: Type-2 (L_2) laws relating intervening variables to

Table 2.1
The Logical Situation of Mentalistic Concepts in Psychology

Meaning 1: Ties to causes/predictors		Meaning 3: Dictionary definition		Meaning 2: Ties to behavior
Number of reinforcements	L_2	Habit	L_3	Probability of response
Score on IQ test	L_2	Intelligence	L_3	School success
Extra twenty-first chromosome	L_2	Down's syndrome	L_3	Low IQ, affectionate behavior
Observations of how parents treat children	L_2	Style of parenting	L_3	Quality of subsequent adjustment
Stressors: Daily hassles, personal conflicts, catastrophes	L_2	Stress	L_3	Reactions: Alarm, resistance, recoil, exhaustion
Imagery ratings in a separate test	L_2	Imagery	L_3	Recall score in later experiment
Behavior in diagnostic interview	L_2	Specific psychological disorder	L_3	Prognosis, therapeutic success
Family after children are grown and gone	L_2	Empty nest	L_3	Seek new challenge or sink deeper roots?
Frustration? Hunger/prey? Threat/fear?	L_2	Aggression	L_3	Behavior intended to harm another person

Note: The general pattern is:

Independent variable———L_2———Concept———L_3———Dependent variable.

independent variables and Type-3 (L_3) laws relating intervening variables to dependent variables. Thus, the formula presented earlier,

Independent variable ———L_1——— Dependent variable,

became:

Independent ——— L_2 ——— Intervening ——— L_3 ——— Dependent
variable   variable   variable.

Actually William James anticipated the intervening-variable approach. He mentioned "the manner in which mental life seems to intervene between impressions made from without upon the body and reactions of the body upon the outer world" (James 1890a, 1:6). And he suggested that "the whole neural organism [is] but a machine for converting stimuli into reactions; and the intellectual part of our life is knit up with but the middle or 'central' portion of the machine's operations" (2:372).

Intervening Variables in Psychology's Two Sciences
The situations of intervening variables differ when these concepts figure in the Type-S laws of experimental psychology and the Type-P laws of correlational psychology. In experimental psychology, the formula is,

Environmental ——— L_2 ——— Intervening ——— L_3 ——— Behavior.
conditions   variable

Intervening variables link behavior to conditions in the present situation or past experiences of organisms.

In correlational psychology the formula is,

Property of ——— L_2 ——— Intervening ——— L_3 ——— Behavior.
organism   variable

Intervening variables link behavior to such characteristics of organisms as their physical and physiological condition and their knowledge, skills, and emotions, assessed by tests and other measures.

In the psychometric version of correlational psychology, the intervening variables are defined operationally in terms of observations of behavior, most often on a test. The concepts so defined are then taken as predictors of performance in some target situation. Thus, an individual's score on a certain test defines (L_2) that person's intelligence, which provides a prediction (L_3) of his or her success in school. Clinical diagnoses and prognoses follow the same pattern. In a diagnostic interview, samples of behavior define (L_2) a mental disorder, a concept that predicts (L_3) subsequent adjustment and the effectiveness of different therapies.

The examples in table 2.1 reveal that intervening variables, defined in terms of the properties of organisms, occur in many contexts. Sometimes the independent variables are physical and physiological attributes, like body build in Sheldon's (1942) theory of temperament and genetic makeup in Down's syndrome and phenylketonuria. In other cases, the variables that play the role of independent variables in experimental psychology are response-inferred intervening variables—for example, imagery, reinforcer, suprathreshold stimulus, stressor, and style of parenting. Each of these variables is a concept defined by observations that are separate from the studies in which they look like independent variables. In social psychology, the field theory put forth by Kurt Lewin (1938) is an important historical example. The quasi-physical concepts of that theory—valence, vector, tension system, permeability of boundaries, and the rest—are defined by reference to behavior, not in terms of physics.

The Goal of Quantification

One of the ambitions of the science of psychology is to express its L_1, L_2, and L_3 laws numerically. The concepts of intelligence and habit strength will show how the laws of an intervening-variable psychology with that ambition realized might look, in correlational and experimental psychology, respectively—although in both cases the actual laws are less precise than my quantitative statements will suggest.

The concept of intelligence links performance on certain tests to quality of school performance as reflected in a measure like a student's grades. Diagrammatically,

Test
performance————L_2————Intelligence
quotient————L_3————School
performance

Hull's (1943) concept of habit strength, s^Hr, ties learned responses to reinforcement:

Number of
reinforcements————L_2————s^Hr————L_3————Probability of
reaction.

These diagrams show that quantitative laws involving intervening variables require numerical expressions of the L_2 and the L_3 laws. For intelligence, the situation is straightforward: the L_2 law is any of the available formulas for IQ, and the L_3 law is the correlation between IQ and success in school.

For Hull's concept of habit strength, the situation is more complex but identical in format. The L_2 law is an equation that defines that concept as a function of number of reinforcements: $s^Hr = M - M_e^{-iN}$, where M is an upper limit (determined by such variables as the amount and delay of reinforcement) that $s^H r$ approaches; e is 10, the base of the common logarithms; i is a constant, reflecting individual differences; and N is the number of reinforcements. Hull's L_3 law is a threshold model of response evocation, which applies not to $s^H r$ but to $s^E r$, a concept derived from $s^H r$ by including the effects of drive and inhibition.

Meanings of Psychological Concepts

Scientific concepts have no God-given meanings, only those that science creates for them. In psychology, defining operations provide concepts with two useful kinds of meaning (Meaning 1 and Meaning 2; see table 2.1); the absence of such operations leaves another kind (Meaning 3; see table 2.1) without scientific value. Meanings 1 and 2 derive their respective meanings from the participation of a concept in psychology's L_2 and L_3 laws. Meaning 3 is a nonoperational, dictionary meaning that defines a concept in terms of other concepts.

In the case of intelligence, Meaning 1 (sometimes called operational meaning) is that intelligence is what the IQ tests measure. Meaning 2 (sometimes called meaning as significance) is that intelligence is what is reflected by success in school. Meaning 3 is some lexical meaning, such as, "Intelligence is the ability to think abstractly and deal effectively with the environment." Meanings 1 and 2, which connect intelligence to observables, make the concept acceptable to science. Meaning 3 is problematic because it does not specify defining operations; "abstract thinking" and "effective dealing with the environment" are no closer to observation than the concept they define. Meaning 3 is purely verbal, and that definition of intelligence is unacceptable to science until the links of the component concepts to observation are established. Without such connections, mentalistic concepts are checks drawn on an empty epistemic bank account.

Acceptability of Concepts in Psychology

With an exception to be noted in a moment, to be suitable for science, the concepts of psychology must have both Meanings 1 and 2. Lacking either, they cannot survive. An example that Gustav Bergmann used in courses at the University of Iowa fifty years ago describes one of the two roads that constructs may take to conceptual oblivion. In approximately Bergmann's words: I can define a concept, Beta (for Bergmann), as follows: Beta is equal to the square root of the number of hairs on my head (a small number), multiplied by the ratio of my systolic to my diastolic blood pressure. The operational definition of

Beta—its Meaning 1, its L_2 law—is impeccable, but the concept never caught on in psychology because it lacks significance. It has no Meaning 2; there is no L_3 law that ties it to behavior. The potentially more useful concept of empty nest (table 2.1), defined as a family's frame of mind when the last child is grown and gone, is similar. Its operational definition is satisfactory, but its meaning for behavior is unclear: Do parents in an empty nest put down deeper roots or seek new worlds to conquer? Diagrammatically,

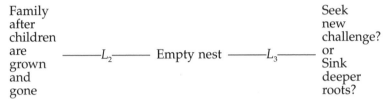

Family after children are grown and gone —L_2— Empty nest —L_3— Seek new challenge? or Sink deeper roots?

The concept of aggression, defined on the dependent variable side as destructive acts intended to bring harm to others, illustrates the other flaw that disqualifies a concept. It has no firm ties to independent variables, probably because there are many different kinds of aggression that appear as reactions to frustration and threat or appear in the process of a search for nourishment. Diagrammatically,

Frustration? Hunger/prey? Threat/fear? —f_2— Aggression —f_3— Behavior intended to harm another person.

A Third Legitimate Variety of Meaning

Although operational definitions succeed in making mentalistic entities legal in the science of psychology, they sometimes come in for criticism because they seem to reduce the explanation of behavior to relationships between single stimuli and responses, a judgment that usually is invalid. In psychological theory, constructs usually behave like agglutinative grammars (e.g., Turkish) that establish complex meanings by adding endings to words. The immediate conceptual precursor to action is a terminal construct that includes the influences of several earlier concepts in an explanatory chain. The classical theories of learning of Guthrie, Hull, Tolman, and even Skinner (Kimble 1985) all followed such a plan.

The most explicitly developed of these theories, that of Clark L. Hull, defined a series of intervening variables, some in terms of physical operations but others in terms of one another. Hull defined a concept "*habit*" operationally, as a function of number of prior reinforcements. He defined another concept, *"drive,"* also operationally, in terms of motivational conditions (food deprivation, for example). Hull then defined a third concept, *"excitatory potential,"* as the joint product of these concepts:

Excitatory potential $= f$(habit) $\times f$(drive),

The next in Hull's chain of intervening variables were two inhibitory constructs: one was a drivelike state, *"reactive inhibition,"* which was an increasing function of the energy requirements of a to-be-learned response. The other, *"conditioned inhibition,"* like a habit, was an increasing function of the number of elicitations of the response that produces reactive inhibition. Hull summed these two forms of inhibition to define the concept *"total inhibition,"* which subtracted from *"excitatory potential"* to produce *"effective excitatory potential"*:

Effective excitatory potential $=$ Excitatory potential $-$ total inhibition.

And so on. Concepts of *"momentary oscillation"* and *"threshold"* (both response-defined intervening variables, suggested by the facts that the strength of behavior varies from time to time, and sometimes a response fails to appear at all) joined with *"effective excitatory potential"* to produce *"momentary effective suprathreshold excitatory potential,"* the concept of which behavior was immediately a function.

Although this cumbersome structure is unattractive because science seeks simplicity, it illustrates two important points: (1) the determination of behavior is complex and the theories required for explanation must also be complex, probably even more complicated than Hullian theory, and (2) the operational criterion for the acceptability of concepts is a bottom-line criterion. In science, concepts can have a useful meaning that derives from their relationships to lower-level concepts. These concepts defined in terms of other concepts are acceptable, however, only if their constituents are traceable to "thing-level" operations.

Different Operations, Different Meanings

Sometimes in different contexts—for example, in psychology's two sciences—different concepts go by the same name, encouraging the mistaken conclusion that they are identical. Vulnerability to cardiac disorder is an example. Its dual status is shown in the following diagrams, which present independent variables, intervening variables, and dependent variables, in that order.

Experimental Psychology

Environmental stress ———— Vulnerability$_1$ ———— Heart disease

Correlational Psychology

Type-A responses ———— Vulnerability$_2$ ———— Heart disease

The important point to note about these diagrams is that although the two concepts of vulnerability go by the same name, Vulnerability$_1$ and Vulnerability$_2$ are different concepts because they are defined in terms of different independent variables.

The Question of Correctness

Can the definition of a concept be right or wrong? Consider the question people ask about alcoholism: Is it a disease, an evil act of will, or a bad habit? The answer to this question has financial consequences. If alcoholism is a disease, therapy for the disorder qualifies for insurance payments; if it is an act of will, it does not; if it is a habit, it depends on whether behavior therapy qualifies, something that differs from time to time and place to place.

The fact that there are arguments over which definition is correct might lead to the conclusion that the debate is about things with substance—that asking whether a man is an alcoholic is like asking whether he has a parrot riding on his shoulder. If that were the case, different definitions would indeed be right or wrong. In actuality, however, the battles over definitions are over concepts, not things. The usefulness of these definitions depends on the degree to which they tie a concept to independent and dependent variables. Putting the concept of alcoholism into a now-familiar diagram will illustrate this point:

Independent variable	*Intervening variable*	*Dependent variable*
Biological cause ————	Alcoholism as a disease	———— Symptoms
Environmental cause ——	Alcoholism as an evil habit	———— Changed behavior
? ————————	Alcoholism as an act of will	———— Personally initiated behavior

This analysis shows that definitions of alcoholism as a disease or as a habit are both acceptable to science because they have the necessary empirical foundations. First, they identify biological and environmental causes: genetics and physiology in the case of alcoholism as a disease; availability of the drug and peer pressure in the case of alcoholism as a habit. Second, they point to observable dependent variables: symptoms in the disease model, changes in behavior compared with the alcoholic's conduct earlier in life in the view of alcoholism as a habit. The definition in terms of willpower is unacceptable because it creates a concept without independent variables. It has only Meaning 3; the personal initiation of behavior is the dictionary equivalent of the concept "will."

The Question of Causality
The notion that psychological concepts have correct definitions often goes hand in hand with the belief that correct definitions are correct because they identify the causes of behavior. This idea reflects an assumption that is deeply rooted in the language of psychology. In a common way of speaking, the causes of behavior are in the traits of individuals: people do this or that because they are ambitious, dirty-minded, over-sexed, or altruistic, and the correct definition is the one that identifies the proper disposition.

Such statements of causality are circular; they violate the fundamental rule that the causes of phenomena must be something other than themselves. Returning to the example of alcoholism, uncontrollable drinking is the major symptom (definition) of alcoholism. Thus, the explanation that says that alcoholism is the cause of George's drinking says nothing more than, "George drinks because he drinks."

The Circle Stays Unbroken
Potentially the explanations in psychology that offer traits as causes are subject to such criticism. The explanatory value of statements such as "Amos feels so worthless because he has a bipolar depressive disorder" is just as empty as "George drinks because he drinks" if the diagnosis of depression rests on nothing more than tests and clinical interviews that reveal Amos' unhappy frame of mind. Such statements of causality are unacceptable because the explanation is the same as what it offers to explain.

To gain acceptability, statements of causality must break the circle. In the general case, there are two possibilities: evidence that (1) ties a concept to environmental antecedents or (2) coordinates the concept to a physiological condition. In the specific case of bipolar disorders, the environmental antecedents might be those that produce learned helplessness; the physiological condition might be levels of serotonin and norepinephrine that are too high or too low.

Proximal and Distal Causes   As this example shows, when an intervening variable (bipolar disorder) is acceptable as a cause of behavior, it is an immediate (*proximal*) cause that has a more remote (*distal*) cause (learned helplessness or level of a neurotransmitter). But distal causes also have causes of their own (uncontrollable punishment or genetics). The causal chain is long or, maybe, endless. In the words of a familiar bit of doggerel: *These fleas have little fleas upon their backs to bite 'em. But the little fleas have littler fleas, and so on, ad infinitum.*

Surplus Meaning   Whatever the dispositional cause suggested for behavior, the common-language words that name it will carry surplus meaning. Many of the debates in the history of psychology have been about such connotations instead of anything with substance. In the field of learning, for example, the central concept is a nameless something that represents enduring changes in behavior produced by practice on some task. Calling it a "habit," "expectancy," "receptor-effector connection," "stimulus-response association," "insight," "reorganized perceptual environment," "deeply processed memory," "altered cognitive map," "dendritic growth," or "improved synaptic transmission" (all of which have been suggested at one time or another) adds nothing to that meaning. What it does do, for anyone who insists on the acceptance of any of these meanings, is to create an obligation to specify the operations that justify insistence on those specific names, something that seems straightforward only for the physiological-sounding terminology.

Complex Reality and the Categories of Psychology

The simple fact that most psychological and biological traits are normally distributed is evidence that behavior is complexly determined. The familiar bell curve is an expression of the effects produced by many independent causes. In that sense, the normal distributions of extroversion and IQs have the same significance as the "chance" distribution of numbers of heads in a series of coin tosses. "Chance" does not mean "uncaused"; it means "complexly caused." Whether, on a given toss, a given coin comes down heads or tails is determined by a host of variables—the force with which the coin was flipped, the height of the toss, the speed with which the coin rotates, the quality of the surface on which it lands—but all of these causes, acting independently on many different coins, produce a set of outcomes that approximates a normal distribution.

The Concept of Stress
To illustrate this complexity with a psychological example, consider the painful state that we call stress. Years of research on that condition have revealed that it is caused by hundreds of specific stressors (independent variables) and expressed in probably as many specific behavioral stress reactions (dependent variables). The causes range from "cataclysmic events" (environmental threats produced by such catastrophes as floods, earthquakes, and war), through "personal stressors" (pressures that are internal to the individual, like those brought on by entering adolescence, loss of employment, and divorce) to "background stressors" (the hassles of everyday life: the nagging irritations at home, school, and work that sabotage existence). Similarly, there are hundreds of stress reactions that fall into two major categories: physiological and psychological. The psychological reactions to stress (table 2.2) fall naturally into three divisions that correspond to the "knowing-feeling-doing" categories introduced in chapter 1.

The Concept of Motivation
When the logical status of the concept "motivation" is spelled out in detail, that construct turns out to have features resembling those described for stress. The similarities include a multiplicity of causes and reactions and a set of theoretical intervening processes that fit the Aristotelian categories. The usual definitions of motivation treat that concept as a disposition that prompts an organism (1) to pay attention to objects of a certain class, to (2) experience an emotional excitement of a certain quality when perceiving such an object, and (3) to act in a certain manner in regard to it. These three components of motivation are cognition, affect, and reaction tendencies, listed in that order.

The placement of cognition, affect, and reaction tendency in this context, which is familiar territory for experimental psychology, suggests that affect and cognition converge on reaction tendencies in the elicitation of behavior. As William James expressed it, "The willing [doing] department of our nature, in short, dominates both the conceiving [knowing] department and the feeling department; or, in plainer English, [feeling and] thinking are only there for behavior's sake" (James 1887). This relationship is a simple version of the cumulative pattern I described in presenting Clark Hull's treatment of the complexities of learned behavior.

Somatotypes and Personality
The knowing-feeling-doing categories also lie behind the popular stereotype relating physique to personality. Cognition dominates the psyche of the fragile, stringbean intellectual; affect is in charge of the fat,

Table 2.2
Some Stress Reactions

Physiological Reactions	Psychological Reactions
Pounding heart	*Intellect/cognition*
Dryness of mouth and throat	Confusion
	Inability to concentrate
Frequent need to urinate	Feelings of unreality
Diarrhea, indigestion, vomiting	Vivid "flashbulb memories" of experience
	Repression of the traumatic experience
Premenstrual tension, missed menstrual cycle	*Emotion/affect*
Sweating	Irritability, hyperexcitation
Loss of or excessive appetite	Depression
Insomnia	Floating anxiety, fear without knowing fear of what
Posttraumatic stress disorder	Tension and alertness, the feeling of being keyed up
	Fatigue, loss of the joy of living
Migraine headache	Nightmares
Increased blood pressure, cardiac disorders	Hostility
	Guilt at having survived while others perished
Vulnerability to infection	*Behavior/reaction tendency*
	Increased smoking
	Increased use of legal drugs
	Drug addiction
	Trembling, nervous tics
	Bruxism (grinding the teeth)
	Hypermobility (restless moving about)
	High-pitched nervous laughter
	Stuttering and other speech difficulties
	Accident proneness

Source: Selye (1976)

jolly-then-blue person; reaction tendencies monopolize the lives of the bold, muscular, take-charge individuals. This bit of common wisdom has real, but limited, validity.

In 1942, William Sheldon reported the results of a study of the relationship between body type and temperament. He began by identifying three dimensions of physique: *endomorphy* (plumpness), *mesomorphy* (muscularity), and *ectomorphy* (thinness). Then he identified three varieties of temperament: *viscerotonia* (relaxed, gentle, comfort seeking), *somatotonia* (action oriented, bold), and *cerebrotonia* (restrained, self-centered, intellectual). Finally, he correlated ratings of individuals on these two sets of variables and found that body structure and temperament were related, as would be expected by the common stereotype: endomorphy with viscerotonia, mesomorphy with somatotonia, and ectomorphy with cerebrotonia. Sheldon's correlations were substantial—in the neighborhood of +.80, probably because he made all of the ratings himself. Later studies have obtained correlations that are positive but weaker—more like +.30.

Broader Implications

The most comfortable concepts for psychology are grounded in biology. Familiar examples include the primary colors that are functions of different receptors or neural processes, Down's syndrome that is associated with a chromosomal aberration, and receptive and expressive aphasia that occur as by-products of dysfunction of Wernicke's and Broca's areas of the brain. Although research in physiological psychology suggests that the categories of cognition, affect, and reaction tendency may have such foundations, the details remain to be worked out.

Practical Usefulness of Analysis

In the meantime, psychology would profit by making better use than it does of those categories. For example, the fashionable disposition that psychology refers to as a person's "self-concept" is partly cognitive (self-knowledge), partly affective (self-esteem), and partly a reaction tendency (self-efficacy). Instead of acknowledging these nuances, however, the literature on the topic tends to lump them all together, sometimes as an explicit rejection of analysis. That mistaken philosophy clouds scientific understanding and misses an important point for practice. The different therapies that might be used to help you strengthen your self-concept have different consequences. Cognitive therapy has the power to alter how you know yourself; existential/ humanistic therapy seeks to strengthen your self-esteem; behavior therapy may improve self-efficacy by reinforcing you for competent behavior. A complete therapy would accomplish all of these goals and attend to the organization of these components as an important aspect of an individual's self-concept.

This mention of organization is a reminder of another point. The dissection of a concept into its constituents does not prohibit recognition of the wholeness of behavior. Instead, it shifts the emphasis to a concern for the organizational processes that create these wholes. Indeed, it is impossible to talk rationally about the wholes of anything (e.g., the self-concept) without some grasp on what it is that is being organized.

The Vast Territory of Psychology
In a wider context, these three ingredients of mental functioning combined with the three main kinds of evidence to which psychology appeals for understanding—psychometric, biological and environmental—produce the grid in table 2.3, which is a rough map of a good bit of the territory of psychology. The entries are topics that are fairly clear examples of one ingredient studied by one particular method.

Scientific Implications
The complexity created by the recognition that psychological concepts are produced by many antecedents and expressed in many ways has two important consequences for the science of psychology.

First, it means that psychology's simplest laws, relating single aspects of behavior to single independent variables, whether they come from experiments or correlations, are doomed to triviality. The number of variables responsible for any act is so large that the individual laws relating any single one of them to any particular response will account

Table 2.3
Location of a Selection of Topics in the Discipline of Psychology

Focus of interest and investigation	Psychological Categories		
	Cognition (Thinking)	Affect (Feeling)	Reaction tendency (Doing)
Psychometric	Scholastic aptitude, Intelligence, self-concept, assessment of creativity, thought disorder, obsession	Emotionality, introversion, type A persona, self-esteem, assessment of human motives, affective disorder, anxiety	Mechanical aptitude, steadiness, self-presentation, dexterity, handedness, Tourette's syndrome, compulsion
Biological	Genetics of intelligence, neurology of memory, evolution of communication, perseveration deficit	Genetics of temperament, biology of instinct, neurochemistry of emotion, hyperphagia, polydipsia	Genetics of physique, physiological arousal and performance, neurology of involuntary and voluntary acts, Parkinson's disease
Environmental	Cognitive therapy, paired-associate learning, cognitive dissonance, social cognition, information processing	Systematic desensitization, conditioned emotions, emotional conflict, social influence, learned helplessness	Aversive therapy, acquisition of motor skill, motor conflict, social action, reaction time, machine-operator compatibility

for only tiny fractions of the variance in behavior. For that reason, complaints about research that obtains only small effects may be unjustified; they may fail to recognize that such studies are unusually well controlled.

Looking at the inevitability of small effects of single variables from another point of view shows that this cloud has a silver lining. It resolves a paradox of common sense. The wisdom of the ages is not notably consistent. It claims that people are about the same the whole world over but also that every person is unique. If the major message of this book is correct, both of these folk sayings are correct. People everywhere are all the same, in the sense that their behavior obeys a set of common laws. At the same time, however, uniqueness is inevitable because the contexts in which these laws operate are so varied that no two individuals turn out to be the same.

In terms that are specific to psychology, this reasoning resolves the conflict over nomothetic and ideographic lawfulness. The laws of behavior assign people to any of an infinite number of locations on innumerable psychological dimensions; the number of combinations of positions on dimensions is astronomical. As a result, the probability that two individuals will be identical is vanishingly small. Uniqueness (ideographic lawfulness) is an expected consequence of the countless contexts in which the general (nomothetic) laws operate.

The second consequence is that the complexity of the determination of behavior is that the number of such Type-1 laws required to explain any psychological phenomenon will be unmanageably large. Without considering the physiology of concepts (in order to keep the discussion manageable), suppose that some phenomenon in psychology has N causes and M behavioral manifestations. The number of Type-1 laws required to state all of the implied relationships will be $N \times M$. If $N = 30$ and $M = 20$ (not an unreasonable assumption, as the previous discussion of the topic, stress, revealed), the number of Type-1 laws is $30 \times 20 = 600$. The replacement of the Type-1 laws with Type-2 and Type-3 laws reduces the number of laws required to $N + M$—that is, N Type-2 laws relating the concept to independent variables, plus M Type-3 laws, relating the concept to dependent variables: $30 + 20 = 50$, rather than 600, without the use of intervening variables.

Summary and Conclusions

The earliest psychology to play according to the scientific rules was J. B. Watson's classical (radical) behaviorism, but its game plan was too conservative. It excluded from the science everything subjective, including psychology's then-standard subject matter, mental states, and its method, introspection. This reduction of psychology to stimuli and responses raised questions: What has happened to the mind and consciousness in this strangely antipsychological psychology? Have the dignity and warmth of human life perished in the icy waters of behaviorism? Operational (methodological) behaviorism, especially the versions of it developed by Tolman, Hull, and Spence, gave psychology the answer to these questions. It showed psychology how to be both a science and a psychology, by treating mental concepts as intervening variables that bridge the gap between independent and dependent variables.

In experimental psychology, intervening variables connect environmental causes and behavior. In correlational psychology, they link measures of the attributes of organisms to behavior. The intervening-variable strategy replaces the Type-1 laws, which relate independent and dependent variables directly, with Type-2 laws, relating independent variables to intervening variables, and Type-3 laws, relating intervening variables to dependent variables. In doing so, the intervening-variable approach decreases the number of laws required to describe the knowledge of a phenomenon. The most powerful of the Type-2 and Type-3 laws are quantitative statements of numerical regularities.

Operationism began as an analysis of the meanings of scientific concepts. In psychology, it produced a recognition that the concepts of the discipline have three different kinds of meaning. Meaning 1, operational meaning, defines concepts in terms of their relationships to independent variables. If they meet that operational criterion, Meaning 1 can be arbitrary:

> "When I use a word," Humpty Dumpty said, in a rather scornful tone, "it means what I choose it to mean—neither more nor less."
> "The question is," said Alice, "whether you can make words mean so many different things."
> "The question is," said Humpty Dumpty, "which is to be master—that's all." Alice was too puzzled to say anything. (Carroll 1954, 185).

Although that argument has a grain of truth, in addition to their Meaning 1 (the only meaning Humpty Dumpty recognizes), acceptable concepts in psychology must have a Meaning 2 that limits the freedom to be arbitrary. Meaning 2 gives concepts significance by establishing their ties to dependent variables. The concepts that survive in the science of psychology have both Meaning 1 and Meaning 2 or are made up of lower-level concepts that possess those meanings.

Most frequently, in common conversation, the meanings of behavioral concepts are dictionary meanings (Meaning 3) that translate a concept into other concepts. Although Meaning 3 often seems to say important things about psychological states and processes ("Intelligence is the ability to think abstractly and to deal effectively with the environment"), intervening variables with only this third kind of meaning are unacceptable to science because there are no operations that tie the concept to observable reality. Certain concepts have a Meaning 4, however, which makes something like Meaning 3 acceptable. In science, concepts form a structure, in which some higher-level concepts are defined by the relationships among lower-level concepts. If these lower-level concepts are operationally defined, the higher-level concepts are legitimate. Otherwise they may do damage to the science because of the surplus meanings carried by their names.

The legitimacy of Meaning 4 makes the intervening-variable approach amenable to extensions of the kind that puts psychology in a position to deal with the complexities of behavior. A particularly useful extension is one proposing that cognition, affect, and reaction tendency, in varying proportions, are ingredients in the recipe for every human act. It appears, in fact, that the whole discipline of psychology is in the business of investigating these Aristotelian attributes with a variety of different methods.

The ability of scientific analysis to handle such intimate matters as an individual's self-concept, in terms that have both theoretical significance and practical importance, shows the potential of the science of psychology for providing a meaningful account of the details of human mental life. If there are aspects of behavior and experience that science cannot handle, there is no way of proving this without giving the scientific way a chance.

Chapter 3

The Structure of the Science

When Tolman offered his new formula for behaviorism in 1922, he suggested that "a true nonphysiological behaviorism is really possible and, when it is worked out, it will be found capable of covering the results of mental tests, objective measurements of memory, animal psychology and everything that was valid in the older introspective psychology." He called his new behaviorism "an offering of peace, not just to the experimental psychologists and animal workers, but also to the clinical psychologists and to the addicts of cognition and of feeling tone" (Tolman 1922, pp. 46–47). Convinced by this argument that psychology can have its cake (mental states) and eat it too (remain a science) by treating psychic qualities as concepts, psychology bought Tolman's intervening-variable approach and logical positivism as its philosophy of science. Teamed up with the presumption that psychology had attained a Newtonian stage in its development, these themes laid the foundation for the development of a new set of comprehensive grand theories, which were the last important expressions of the belief that a unified psychology is possible.

The Era of Grand Theory

All of these new theories employed the hypothetico-deductive method. Such a theory consists of a set of postulates about the subject matter of a science and deductions of the logical consequences of the interrelationships among those postulates. Isaac Newton's physics (Cajori 1947) is the prototype. In Newton's theory, deductions of the implications of just three laws of motion explained such diverse phenomena as the behavior of falling objects, the orbits of the planets, and the ebb and flow of tides. Following that model, the new theories in psychology offered a few basic propositions and harbored the belief that the deductive elaboration of these propositions would explain large segments of behavior. The theories of learning of Guthrie, Hull, and Tolman and Lewin's field theory, which dealt in the main with social action, were the most influential versions of the approach.

To illustrate the method, in their versions of hypothetico-deductive theory, both Hull and Lewin proposed what Hull referred to as a "goal-gradient hypothesis"—the idea that the strength of a tendency to approach a goal increases as an individual comes nearer to that goal. On the basis of this hypothesis and appropriate supporting assumptions, Lewin deduced the counterintuitive fact that prisoners attempt to escape from jail with increasing frequency as the official date of their release draws closer; and Hull explained the order in which rats in a complex maze learn to avoid blind alleys: those closest to the goal are eliminated first, followed in succession by those nearer and nearer to the starting point.

Decline and Fall
Although a multitude of experiments supported their predictions, the grand theories also had shortcomings that led to their rejection. These theories all assumed that their basic principles applied without distortion to the behavior of lower animals and human beings, to infants and older people, to industrialized and primitive societies, and, in all these contexts, to behavior that was manifest and covert, physical and verbal, simple and complex, sane and crazy. The ritualistic exercise of these presumptions produced some dreadful science. In child psychology, it legitimated a rash of experiments that applied the paradigms employed with rats to children—with the expectation that the results would be the same, and if they were not, the sense that the study was defective. In abnormal psychology there was a flood of largely inconclusive attempts to manufacture laboratory analogues of psychopathological phenomena, aimed at the validation of such hypotheses as that the essence of the schizophrenic process is defective stimulus generalization. In experimental psychology, there was a premature standardization of procedures. For example, journal editors rejected studies of the galvanic skin reaction that used interstimulus intervals that were longer (and we now know better) than half a second that had become the sacred norm.

Miniature Systems   Inevitably, there was criticism of these trends in psychology. Soon after World War II, the critics began belittling them as antitheoretical "dust-bowl empiricism," or, less charitably, as "scientism" masquerading as a science. It took about a decade for psychology to admit that there was an element of truth in these charges. With the recognition of that reality, many psychological scientists abandoned grand theorizing and turned to miniature systems designed to handle more limited ranges of phenomena, with more precision. The result of this development was the first of two disasters that befell the science of psychology in the second quarter of the twentieth century.

The triumph of the narrow specialties robbed the discipline of its coherence. Almost no one tried to show that the principles of one system are the same as those of others, and psychology became a shattered discipline, a pursuit without a unifying theme.

Antipositivistic Rebellion   Simultaneously, in some quarters there were growing doubts about psychology's empirical foundation. The awakenings of the 1960s throughout the social sciences led most psychologists to a search for relevance and to commerce with such concepts as imagery, cognition, self-esteem, and consciousness. Psychologists did not yet understand that the intervening-variable approach made those phenomena legitimate for study, and many of them rejected positivism and operationism because of the gossip that, back home in philosophy, they were in trouble.

In part, the consequences of renouncing the ordained methodology were positive. Psychologists began to study once-forbidden topics, such as voluntary action, deep linguistic structures, and real-world memory, with once-outlawed methods such as free recall, self-report, and hypnosis. On balance, however, the consequences of this development were negative. They brought on psychology's second ruinous disaster: they cost the discipline its scientific self-respect.

Some of the psychologists who rebelled against the positivist position abandoned science in favor of undisciplined subjectivism. They turned to common sense, great literature, and private intuition as sources of knowledge for psychology. They accepted personal dispositions rather than external causes as the explanations of behavior. They preferred holism to analysis in their theories (Kimble 1984). Their literature was an exhibition of jargon/substance and feeling/thinking ratios that are more appropriate for art criticism than science. Psychology still suffers from the two misfortunes that came to it in that period: fragmentation of the discipline and a regression to antiscientific practice.

Orienting Commitments

The unattractive situation in psychology today suggests that the time has come to give grand theorizing another chance: to find the principles, if they exist, that hold the field together and to show their application to subject matters beyond the narrow specialties. This book presents a sketch of how that unified psychology could look.

The approach I present here might be called *functional behaviorism*. As we saw in chapter 1, behaviorism is a necessary consequence of the decision to be an empirical science. The functionalist perspective acknowledges that behavior is the product of evolution, which preserves for posterity the fittest conduct of a species, along with its fittest physical structures and physiological functions. This commitment has sweeping implications.

First, the agents of behavior produced by the evolutionary process are organisms; thus, the laws of psychology must be compatible with biology. This is not the same as an endorsement of reductionism— the assumption that the laws of psychology must be translatable into physiology. It is the more modest claim that the laws of psychology must not conflict with biological truth.

A behavioristic psychology that keeps an eye on biology has certain practical advantgages. As I noted in a talk almost fifty years ago, nothing forces psychology into bed with physiology: "Although all behavior probably has its neurophysiological aspects . . . I can conceive of a psychology based on stimulus and response events entirely, one in which the existence of an organism is a completely unimportant fact. The scientific account will, after all, deal with behavior in the abstract. Such a science no more needs to refer to the organism than the science of gravitation needs to refer to stones or to the Leaning Tower of Pisa" (Kimble 1953, p. 158). This argument is reasonable in principle but tilts at windmills.

Not long after I gave that talk, I lost an argument about the issue to George Miller, whom I met for the first time when I went from Brown to Harvard to hear the first of B. F. Skinner's William James Lectures that became the book *Verbal Behavior* (1957). As George and I were getting acquainted, I expressed the prejudice above, but Miller did not buy it. His comment was something like, "If you want to play psychology by those rules, you obviously don't want to play the game for keeps. The situation is like solitaire. There are rules against looking at the cards you might turn over before you decide on one. But, there will be critical moments when the best thing to do will be to break that rule and peek."

The second implication is that human conduct evolved in response to the demands of the physical environment. This history is responsible for important characteristics of behavior. For example, some real-world happenings, such as day and night and spring, summer, fall, and winter, occur in cycles. Organisms are sensitive to these periodicities, and the consequences are evident in numerous diurnal rhythms, winter hibernation, and seasonal affective disorders. Some physical events, such as the day-night cycle, are uncontrollable; there is nothing that evolving organisms can do to regulate them. Others, such as the availability of the materials needed to maintain life, can be controlled. It should come as no surprise to learn that different behavioral mechanisms evolved to deal with these realities.

This emphasis on the physical environment does not deny the existence or importance of the so-called psychological or perceptual environment emphasized by many social psychologists. It is true, of course, that, when people differ in their perceptions of a situation, their behavior can be very different. It is a mistake, however, to think of the perceptual environment as an independent variable. It is an intervening variable—actually two different kinds of intervening variables.

In one (Type-S) sense, the concept of psychological environment stands between a collection of causal environmental independent variables and behavior:

Physical environment
Internal environment ——Psychological environment———Behavior
Past experience

The different conceptions of the world (psychological environments) that exist in different cultures are possible for every culture. The basic laws of behavior do not differ from one society to another, but, operating in different physical and social climates, they lead to different outcomes.

In a second (Type-P) sense, the concept of psychological environment links interpretive responses (e.g., verbal reports) and subsequent behavior:

Responses to
the
physical   ——Psychological environment———Behavior
environment

In this sense, psychological environment is like "style of parenting" and the Lewinian concepts of valence, vector, and permeability of boundaries mentioned in chapter 2 (p. 22) It is an intervening variable that looks like an independent variable, and some psychologists mistakenly think of it as such.

The third point is that the evolutionary process is cumulative; it leaves newly evolved organisms with talents of their ancestors, although in every species above the level of one-celled organisms, these atavistic capabilities, although present, will be hidden by a veneer of newer acquisitions called "emergences." This extravagance of nature is adaptive because sometimes the more primitive abilities come in handy. They are like the habits retained in adulthood from early stages of individual development. For very simple problems, the very simple strategies of childhood are appropriate, to the point where the sophisticated habits of maturity may even allow problems to go unsolved (Stevenson, Iscoe, and McConnell 1955). Freud's concept of regression in the service of the ego is another recognition of the adaptive usefulness of immature responses. This assumption also encourages the hope that there are very general laws of behavior that apply on every rung of the phylogenetic ladder.

Axioms of Action: An Overview

Beginning in the next section of this chapter, this book develops the implications of five hypotheses that I offer as psychology's equivalents of Newton's laws of motion. In anticipation of details to come, I begin here with a summary, a brief sketch that will be useful because these principles operate together. Later, when I deal with them separately, there will be times when discussing one of them will require a mention of another.

Hypothesis 1: Behavior is the joint product of relatively enduring potentials for and relatively temporary instigations to action. Potentials are the abiding characteristics of individuals. Each of us carries around a host of unexpressed potentials for (often opposite) behavior that may or may not gain expression, depending on the situation. When someone asks a personal question, you have the potentials to lie or tell the truth about yourself. When you are faced with physical danger, you may collapse in fear or strike out against it. When you see someone in trouble, you may offer assistance or avoid involvement. The responses that occur in such situations, and their strengths if they do, depend on the circumstances of the moment—that is, existing instigations. "Instigation" is a useful word, referring to factors in the individual and the environment that energize potentials or suppress them.

This potential-instigation principle is psychology's version of Newton's first two laws of motion. Law I describes potential physical actions that may or may not occur: "Every body continues in its state of rest, or of uniform motion in a right line, unless it is compelled to change that state by forces [instigation] impressed upon it" (Cajori 1947, p. 13). In psychology the key expression is "uniform motion" because organisms are always doing something; even single neurons fire spontaneously. Law II describes how instigation determines the strength of such actions as occur: "The change of motion is proportional to the motive force impressed; and is made in the direction of the right line in which the force is impressed" (Cajori 1947, p. 13).

Hypothesis 2: Behavior is a blend of just two ways of dealing with the environment: adapting to events that organisms cannot control and coping when control is possible. This principle is a consequence of physical reality.

There are two kinds of happenings in the world. Some events occur in sequence, no matter what you try to do about them: at least a little pain is inevitable once the dentist picks up the drill; "Ol' man river he just keeps rollin' along." Others are events where what we do has consequences: work a little harder, and you solve the problem that you have been struggling to master; "Get a little drunk and you land in jail."

Hypothesis 3: Behavior happens when instigation raises a potential to a threshold. Lesser instigations may have effects, but they stay latent until instigation brings them to a threshold. The straws that ruin personal relationships, like those that break the camel's back, are effective because of what they are adding on to.

Hypothesis 4: Behavior is under the simultaneous control of opponent processes of excitation and inhibition. The smooth flow of the baseball pitcher's arm is the expression of an elaborate interaction between opposed muscle groups, one of which relaxes (is inhibited) when the other contracts (is excited). The functioning of a civilized society requires people to curb (inhibit) the urges (excitation) toward hostile and indecent behavior that exist in all of us. This principle is psychology's version of Newton's third law of motion: "To every action there is always opposed an equal reaction: or, the mutual reactions of two bodies upon each other are always equal, and directed to contrary parts" (Cajori 1947, p. 13).

Hypothesis 5: The master plan that guides behavior is hierarchical organization. If I begin a sentence, "Spare the rod . . . " and ask you to read my mind and complete it as I intended to, I have provided you with an organizing plan that makes it likely that you will respond, "and spoil the child." Although these organizations are usually adaptive, they sometimes lead to error. Perhaps the sentence I began was, "Spare the rod and use positive reinforcement in dealing with a child."

These axioms are not my invention or even Isaac Newton's. They are common and time-honored Western ways of thinking—the salient landmarks of the intellectual environment in which the sciences have been evolving for millennia. Most of them appeared in Aristotle.

On behavior as potential brought to actuality by instigation, Aristotle noted that "coming-to-be necessarily implies the pre-existence of something which *potentially* 'is', but *actually* 'is not'" (*On Generation and Corruption,* bk. I, chap. 3). "The fulfillment of what exists potentially . . . is motion" (*Physics,* bk. III, chap. 1). And, "These two appear to be the sources [elsewhere Aristotle called them causes] of movement: appetite and mind" (*De Anima,* bk. III, chap. 9). For Aristotle, the concept of motion included growth, degeneration, and locomotion; appetite included sensation, desire, and hope; mind included thought, perception, opinion, and imagination. A common summary gives Aristotle credit for the important notion in this book: that the major human faculties are knowing, feeling, and doing—cognition, affect, and reaction tendencies.

In what appears to be the same distinction as that between coping and adaptation, Aristotle made reference to "the active and passive affections of the soul" (*De Anima*, bk. I, chap. 4). Put generally, "Motion is . . . the fulfillment of what can act and what can be acted on." For example, "Teaching is the activity of a person who can teach [but] the operation is performed *on* some patient" (*Physics*, bk. III, chap. 3). And the two fulfillments may exist in the same person: "A man who is a doctor might cure himself" (*Physics*, bk. I, chap. 9).

The concept of connected processes of excitation and inhibition appeared in numerous references to "contraries." For example, "If there be a movement natural to the soul, there must be a counter-movement to it, and conversely" (*De Anima*, bk. I, chap. 3).

Aristotle's theory of hierarchical organization grew out of a ranking of organisms, from plants, to animals, to human beings, in a scheme where those at successively higher levels had all of the properties of those of lower rank and additional ones as well. Applied to individuals, "the particulars subsumed under the common name [soul] constitute a series, each successive term of which potentially contains its predecessor. . . . Perception is never found apart from the power of self-nutrition. . . . No sense is found apart from that of touch. . . . [Those living things] which possess calculation have all the powers above" (*De Anima*, bk. II, chap. 3).

Behavior: A Function of Potential and Instigation

As William James described the distinction between potential and actual behavior, "Man is born with a tendency to do more things than he has ready-made arrangements for in his nerve-centres. [Most of his performances] must be the fruit of painful study" (James 1890a, 1:113). "The mind, in short, works on the data it receives very much as a sculptor works on his block of stone. In a sense the statue stood there from eternity. But there were a thousand different ones beside it, and the sculptor alone is to thank for having extricated this one from the rest" (1:288).

James also recognized that potentials are enduring attributes of individuals. In the actions that establish them, "We are spinning our own fates. . . . Nothing we ever do is, in strict scientific literalness, wiped out. Of course, this has its good side as well as its bad one. As we become permanent drunkards by so many separate drinks, so we become saints in the moral, and authorities and experts in the practical and scientific spheres, by so many acts and hours of work (1:127).

James employed a now-rejected neural model as an explanation for that permanence: "[The brain] is like the great commutating switch-board at a central telephone station" (1:27). Its operation is in five steps: (a) A stimulus excites a sense organ adequately for a current to pass to a sensory nerve; (b) the sensory nerve is traversed; (c) the sensory current is transformed into a motor current; (d) the motor nerve is traversed; (e) the motor current excites a muscle to contract (1:88). "The currents, once in, must find a way out. In getting out they leave their traces in the paths which they take. . . . A path once traversed by a nerve-current might be expected to follow the law of most paths that we know, and to be scooped out and made more permeable than before; and this ought to be repeated with each new passage of the current. . . . So nothing is easier than to imagine how, when a current once has traversed a path, it should traverse it more readily a second time" (1:107–109).

Potential Potential versus Realized Potential

To present the implications of the distinction between potential and instigation, it will be useful to distinguish between what I call "potential potentials" and "realized potentials." *Potential potentials* are the range of outcomes that are possible for an individual; *realized potentials* are those that become actual. The underlying idea here resembles the geneticists' concept of "norm of reaction": corresponding to every genotype (potential potential), there is a repertoire of different phenotypes (realized potentials) that can appear in different environments. James made this conception an essential component of his treatment of the concept of self.

> I am often confronted by the necessity of standing by one of my [potential] selves and relinquishing the rest. Not that I would not, if I could, be both handsome and fat and well dressed, and a great athlete, and make a million a year, be a wit and a *bon-vivant,* and a lady killer, as well as a philosopher; a philanthropist, statesman, warrior, and African explorer, as well as a "tone-poet" and saint. But the thing is simply impossible. The millionaire's work would run counter to the saint's; the *bon-vivant* and the philanthropist would trip each other up; the philosopher and the lady-killer could not well keep house in the same tenement of clay. Such different characters may conceivably at the outset of life be alike *possible* to a man. But to make any one of them actual, the rest must more or less be suppressed" (James 1890a, 1:309–310).

The Roles of Instigation

The degree to which these realized potentials translate into action depends on instigation—transient states and circumstances that activate potentials or suppress them. Athletic aptitude and criminality will serve to illustrate the interaction between potential and instigation.

Everyone is born at risk for developing some degree of athletic prowess and expertise in crime. The extent to which people realize these potential potentials depends on their histories: quality of coaching and amount of practice in the case of athleticism; quality of home life and models of delinquency in the case of criminality. Whether the individual with excellent realized athletic potential makes it to the Olympic games or ends up an also ran depends on instigation—a combination of environmental factors (coaches' decisions, strength of the competition, the weather) and internal factors (ambition, determination, laziness, fear of failure) that are not unlike the conditions that determine the extent to which different athletes realize their potentials. Whether the individual with superb realized criminal potential ends up in Attica or leads a more successful life of crime depends on comparable instigations—some of them environmental (the impact of gang membership, the quality of local crime-prevention measures), some of them internal (aggressiveness, greed, guilt, the fear of getting caught).

A Word of Caution

In psychology, the world is never as straightforward as the potential-instigation formula suggests. The most important attribute of the concept "motive" puts it in the category of instigation: motivation provides the energy for behavior. We have already seen, however, that the definition of the concept contains references to cognition and reaction tendencies, which are potentials. The most important attribute of the concept "habit" puts it in the category of realized potential (reaction tendency). Habits are an organism's established ways of doing. But the concept of "functional autonomy"—highly practiced habits become self-perpetuating ends in themselves—suggests that at least some reaction tendencies have elements of instigation (affect). The miser's penny-pinching and the ideas that the patriot or paranoid will fight for are examples.

From Single Neurons to Society

In several of his writings, Kurt Lewin (e.g., 1938) took the position that behavior (B) is a joint function (f) of the properties of the person (P) and the environment (E). He put this thesis quasi-formally, in the equation:

$$B = f(P,E),$$

which expresses the same idea as the proposition that behavior is a function of potentials that are activated or suppressed by instigation. Potentials are personal dispositions, and instigations are influences in the environment, including the internal environment of the person. Thus, a modification of Lewin's equation yields the following translation:

$$B = f(P, I),$$

which says that behavior (B) is a joint function (f) of (usually realized) potential (P) and instigation (I). The paragraphs that follow present this formula in a variety of contexts to show that it applies across the entire territory of psychology, beginning with two very different applications in almost the same words.

As long as a neuron is unstimulated, its membrane maintains an electrical charge called a resting potential. Events that irritate a neuron (instigations) alter this potential, and, up to a point, the greater the irritation is, the greater is the change in potential, an effect that can be detected by appropriate measures of the polarity of the neuron. A stimulus that is strong enough to carry the reaction beyond that point has a markedly different consequence, however. It initiates the discharge called an action potential. Translated into the equation,

$$B = f(P,I),$$

the formula for these facts becomes:

Action potential $= f$(Resting potential, adequate stimulation).

As long as people in a wartime situation are untraumatized, they maintain a predisposition (potential) for a stress reaction. Events (instigations) that irritate them activate this potential, and, up to a point, the greater the irritation is, the greater is the impact on their well-being, an effect that can be detected by appropriate measures of adjustment. Traumata that are strong enough to carry the reaction beyond this point have a markedly different consequence, however. They bring on the symptoms of a stress disorder. In terms of the formula above,

Stress disorder $= f$(Predisposition, precipitating trauma).

These two examples illustrate a general pattern and suggest a further point: the "strong enough" proviso in both examples implies the existence of a threshold that a potential must exceed before it receives expression. In between the responses of a single neuron and the etiology of stress disorders, there are many behavioral processes that fit this general pattern.

Learning versus Performance

The details of the distinction between learning and performance are available in everyday experience. Everyone possesses talents that they exercise only when they are appropriately motivated and free of inhibition. Their healthful habits of jogging or walking become actual behavior only when they have the urge and when they are not too weary. Of all the potential-instigation interactions, this one is the best known and most completely worked out. Over the years, countless laboratory studies have demonstrated the effects of motivation and inhibition on a variety of habits.

Experiments on latent learning produced the classical statement of the distinction, in connection with the type of motivation called incentive. Hungry rats in these experiments explored mazes without receiving a reward for reaching the goal box. During these trials, their performances showed no sign of improvement. When food became available, however, improvement occurred rapidly, suggesting that they had actually been learning but that this learning remained potential (latent) until the animal had an incentive (instigation) to perform.

Demonstrations of spontaneous recovery in conditioning and reminiscence in human motor learning reveal the presence of inhibitory instigations. A conditioned response that has undergone extinction reappears (spontaneously recovers) after a few minutes' rest. A skill acquired with continuous practice gains strength (displays reminiscence) if practice is briefly interrupted. Both phenomena demonstrate the existence of a potential for performance that is greater than just-prior (inhibited) behavior indicated. The following equation includes both of these instigations:

Performance $= f[\text{(Habit)}, \text{(Motivation, inhibition)}]$.

Signal Detectability

Whether an observer reports the presence of a weak stimulus (a "hit") or fails to do so (a "miss") when one is delivered in an experiment on signal detection—and, in the same experiment, whether the individual reports the presence of a signal when there is none (a "false alarm") or reports its absence (a "correct rejection")—depends on the observer's sensitivity to stimulation of the kind employed in the experiment (a potential) and two factors that qualify as instigation: the intensity of the stimulus and the observer's criterion for deciding whether to respond yes or no in such situations. The criterion (bias) is an instigation because it varies with such temporary factors as the patterning of trials with and without stimuli in the experiment and with the rewards and punishments delivered for each of the four possible outcomes.

Observer's report $= f[$(Sensitivity), (Criterion, stimulus intensity)$]$.

Memory

The tip-of-the-tongue experience provides a vivid example of the point under discussion here. As William James described it:

> Suppose we try to recall a forgotten name. The state of our consciousness is peculiar. There is a gap therein; but no mere gap. It is a gap that is intensely active. A sort of wraith of the name is in it, beckoning us in a given direction, making us at moments tingle with a sense of closeness and then letting us sink back without the longed-for term. If wrong names are proposed to us, this singularly definite gap acts immediately so as to negate them. They do not fit the mould. And the gap of one word does not feel like the gap of another, all empty of content as both might seem necessarily to be when described as gaps. (James 1890a, 1:251)

Contemporary psychology treats this phenomenon in terms of a distinction between accessibility and availability of memories. A recollection that is on the tip of the tongue exists as an engram (memory trace). It is potentially available but accessible only with the aid of instigation of the sort that is provided by a cue that might be provided by a hint:

Recall $= f$(Engram, cue).

Problem Solving

People face the problems of the world with rule-of-thumb solutions that are sometimes called heuristics. For example, when selecting someone to fill a position of responsibility, choose a proved winner because past performance is the best predictor of future behavior. On multiple-choice tests, when you do not know the answer, select the longest alternative because it takes more words to say something right than to say something wrong. Classical experiments (Luchins 1942) have shown that such mental sets (an old name for heuristics) are easy to establish and that, depending on their appropriateness, they may aid or interfere with problem solving.

Success/failure $= f$(Heuristic, problem features).

Language

In psycholinguistics, verbal expression and comprehension travel in opposite directions on a two-way street. The creation of a sentence requires the speaker to transform materials in deep linguistic structures (potential) into a perceptible surface structure that has a form determined by the communicative situation (instigation). The understanding of that same sentence requires the listener to perform linguistic processing in the reverse direction. For these two cases, a single formula will do:

Expression/comprehension = f(Deep structure, communicative occasion).

Intelligence

Human fluid intelligence is a genetic potential potential—actually a collection of potentials because measured intelligence is composed of subtraits. The environment determines the extent to which this genetic endowment becomes the realized potential called crystallized intelligence. Intelligent behavior is the manifestation of this realized potential in response to situations. For example, what we call wisdom is the quality that behavior based on crystallized intelligence acquires with years of practice. It takes two equations to express these ideas:

Crystallized intelligence = f(Fluid intelligence, environment).

Intelligent behavior = f(Crystallized intelligence, situation).

Freudian Dream Analysis

Freud's distinction between the manifest and latent content of a dream—the difference between a dream as it is experienced and its underlying meaning—is another example that will be familiar. The dream, as a person remembers it, is its latent meaning dressed up in the masquerade clothing supplied by a censor, symbolism, and repression at the time of recall:

Manifest dream content = f(Latent content, "dream work").

Antisocial Behavior

The violence that human beings inflict on one another to express anti-racial attitudes is a product of an underlying potential (prejudice) and situations (instigation) that enable violence by removing the restraints that normally inhibit such behavior:

Racial violence = f(Prejudice, permissive situation).

People violate the social norms in situations where the possibility for personal gain is strong enough to override their moral sensitivities:

Immoral conduct = f(Moral knowledge, possible personal gain).

Structure of a Model

Figure 3.1 presents a scheme that summarizes the argument of this book. It reviews much of the content of the previous chapters and looks ahead to topics developed in later chapters. It is not a causal diagram but a depiction of how a science of psychology might construct an accounting of animal activities. The entries at the top of the figure are a reminder of the types of lawfulness that relate the independent, intervening, and dependent variables in psychology. The entries lower down spell out some of the details.

The Origins of Action

The best way to read the figure is to begin by noting that behavior—which incidentally, but importantly, includes physiological reactions—happens when the momentary value of a realized potential exceeds a

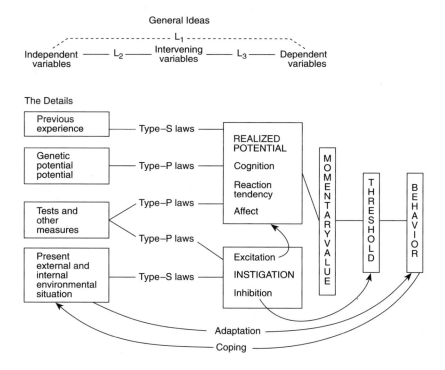

Figure 3.1
A New Formula for Behaviorism
This outline of the structure of a comprehensive science of psychology unites the two sciences shown in figure 1.1. The layout is logically, not temporally or causally, sequential.

threshold. This momentary value is the product of the interaction between a realized potential and the excitatory functions of instigation triggered by the situation of the moment—again, incidentally but importantly, including the internal biological environment as well as external circumstances. I am tentatively proposing that the excitatory and inhibitory functions of instigation operate separately: excitation on realized potential in determining its momentary value and inhibition on reaction thresholds. The two arrows from situation to behavior and from behavior to situation represent the two processes introduced as the second axiom above and discussed in more detail in chapter 4: adaptation, which occurs in situations where behavior leaves the environment unchanged, and coping, which occurs when the behavior of organisms can alter the environment.

Psychology's Two Disciplines
The two scientific disciplines of psychology differ in their choices of the independent variables represented by the entries on the left in figure 3. 1. Experimental psychology deals with the Type-S laws that connect behavior to present situations (instigation) and the previous experience that determined a potential. For example, traditional experimental psychology looked at such responses as reaction time as the joint outcome of sensitivity (a potential) and such variables as stimulus intensity and whether the subject in the reaction-time experiment received a warning signal just before a trial began (instigations). The classical theories of learning attempted to determine how realized potentials increased with practice and how the expression of these potentials changed with changes in such instigations as the kind of stimulation (stimulus generalization), incentive (latent learning), and inhibition (extinction and spontaneous recovery).

Correlational psychology is in the business of predicting behavior on the basis of the Type-P laws that tie behavior to a variety of attributes of organisms—once more including, incidentally but importantly, assessments of the physiological and inherited potentials of the individual. Correlational psychology assumes, of course, that realized potentials have causes and that the extent to which these potentials become manifest depends on situations, but it introduces these conceptions to the science of psychology from observations of the attributes of organisms.

Recent progress in psychology has shown that its two disciplines support each other. For example, experimental psychology joins its correlational sibling when the concepts of psychometric psychology serve as moderator variables in calculations of the interactions between the influences of environmental variables, like task complexity or training method, and individual-difference variables, like anxiety or intelligence. Correlational psychology turns experimental when it deals with trait-situation interactions or, more generally, with the question of the relative importance of situations (one contributor to instigation) and dispositions (a common synonym for potential) in the determination of behavior.

Summary and Conclusions

The scientific explanations of phenomena are demonstrations that they are deductive consequences of a set of hypotheses. Newton's physics is the classical example of this hypothetico-deductive method.

In the second quarter of this century, psychology developed a number of "grand theories" of this type. Although these theories had successes, they also had certain faults that led psychology to abandon them, most often in favor of smaller theories covering more limited areas of content. These minisystems bought precision but at the price of relevance. Many psychologists found this bargain unsatisfactory, and they gave up both the miniature theories and the philosophy of science that gave rise to them.

My reaction to this history is that the rejection of grand theorizing may have been premature, because the data of psychology appear to display patterns that appear across a wide range of behavior. This book presents the outline of a theory of this type, taking an approach that I have called functional behaviorism. The criterion of empiricism means that a science of psychology must be some species of behaviorism. The functional outlook promises generality for the theory within cultures and across a range of species. It rests on these orienting ideas:

- Behavior is the product of organic evolution. The actions of organisms in the world today are those that are adaptive.
- Behavior evolved to meet the demands of the physical environment. The so-called psychological environment is a useful intervening variable, a product of an interaction between the physical environment and other causal independent variables.
- The agents of behavior are organisms. Psychological laws must conform to the knowledge of biology.

My hypothetical axioms of action are the following:

- Behavior is the joint product of relatively enduring *potentials* for, and relatively more temporary *instigation* to, action.
- Behavior is a blend of just two ways of dealing with the environment: *adapting* to events that organisms cannot control and *coping* when control is possible.

- Behavior happens when the strength of a potential exceeds a threshold.
- Behavior is under the simultaneous control of *excitation* and *inhibition.*
- The master plan that guides behavior is *hierarchical organization.*

In this chapter, I have shown that the potential-instigation formula applies in contexts ranging from action potentials in the single neuron to pathological reactions brought on by stress. This interaction is central to my theoretical framework. Many of the implications of this framework will be developed in the remaining chapters of this book.

Chapter 4
Two Forms of Adjustment

For our prehistoric ancestors, the world contained two kinds of objects and occasions: good ones that provided the resources that were required for living and bad ones that threatened security. The changes in behavior that came with evolution served to deal with these realities, and human beings in the world today maintain the same distinction. In ordinary speech, the good things are honor, praise, reward, and good luck; the bad ones are disgrace, punishment, reproof, and misfortune. In psychology, the good things are Thorndike's (1911) satisfiers, Lewin's (1938) objects with positive valence, and learning theory's positive reinforcers. The bad things are Thorndike's annoyers, Lewin's objects with negative valence, and learning theory's negative reinforcers.

Adaptation or/and Coping

Some of these positive and negative events occur without warning. The announcement of your election to an honorific society may take you totally by surprise; the news that you have lost your job because of a very secret reorganization of your company may come out of nowhere. Usually, however, such significant events have signals. A letter from an influential person in your profession hinted that your accomplishments have not gone unnoticed; a series of dismissals and retirements earlier in the year were warnings of unhappy things to come.

Signaled or not, the happenings just mentioned are ones over which you had no control. More often what you do has consequences. Build a better mousetrap, and the world beats a path to your doorway. Laugh and the world laughs with you; cry and you cry alone.

Organisms deal with controllable and uncontrollable events in different ways. In situations where control is possible, they change the world to satisfy their needs. In situations where control is lacking, they change themselves to meet the demands of the environment. I shall refer to these two methods of adjustment as *coping,* when control is possible, and *adaptation,* when it is not. "Coping" and "adaptation" are not evaluative terms. Either of them may be successful or unsuccessful.

In his discussion of the concept of the self, William James made a similar distinction: "If we divide all possible physiological acts into *adjustments* [adapting] and *executions* [coping], the nuclear self would be the adjustments; and the less intimate, more shifting self . . . would be the executions" (James 1890a, 1:302). These ideas are also similar to those that Piaget (1952) employed in his description of the processes by which children adjust to their environments. Children's first responses to intellectual challenge are assimilation, the incorporation of information into existing cognitive structures—by distorting it if necessary. For the baby, objects in the mouth are things to suck, whether the object is a nipple, a thumb, or the tail of the family cat. When assimilation is maladaptive, the result is accommodation, a reorganization of cognitive systems to provide a better match to actuality.

In Piaget's theory, assimilation plays the role that I assigned to coping (controlling information, so that it fits one's mental structures), and accommodation serves the purposes of adaptation (altering those structures when they do not correspond to reality). An important point in this interpretation is that it gives coping priority over adaptation. Assimilation continues until the evidence forces the individual to accommodate.

Translated into the language I am using here, that last idea is that signals predict pleasant or unpleasant things to come, for which adaptation is an automatic reaction after their arrival; but those same signals also prompt coping reactions that, made soon enough, increase the likelihood of positive events and nullify the negative. Thus, most behavior is a blend of adaptation and coping: the signals of inevitabilities produce reactions that increase or decrease the likelihood that the signaled events will happen. For many people, the signs of spring are warnings of hay fever—so they take appropriate medication to minimize those miseries. The first sip of the evening cocktail promises a comfortable sense of well-being, unless you take too many—so you order refills but limit their number. A certain look on mother's face means punishment—so the naughty child smiles and apologizes.

Contingencies and Consequences

In another way of speaking, the relationships between signals and events define two contingencies. Neglecting for the moment the probabilistic nature of the concept, a *contingency* is an if-then relationship between events. Those over which a person has no control are stimulus-stimulus contingencies: if $stimulus_1$, then $stimulus_2$ (if lightning, then thunder). Those where control is possible are response-consequence (or outcome) contingencies (if more study, then better grade). Thus, another way to put the main idea in this chapter is to say that the behavior of organisms is a blend of *adapting* based on stimulus-stimulus contingencies and *coping* based on response-consequence contingencies.

Classical and Instrumental Conditioning

Experiments on classical and instrumental (operant) conditioning are laboratory realizations of these two contingencies: stimulus-stimulus contingencies in classical conditioning and response-consequence contingencies in instrumental conditioning. In classical conditioning, the conditioned stimulus (CS) and unconditioned stimulus (US) come on in a certain order no matter what the subject does, and organisms learn to adapt. In instrumental conditioning, the delivery of positive reinforcers and the withholding of negative reinforcers are contingent on the subject's responses, and organisms acquire the coping skills that favor positive and lessen negative outcomes.

During the early years of research on classical and instrumental conditioning, psychologists treated them as a single process. Later, however, many theorists proposed that they are different in the kinds of behavior that they influence. According to such theorizing, classical conditioning modifies involuntary responses, especially responses of the autonomic nervous system, elicited by identifiable stimuli. Instrumental conditioning modifies voluntary responses of the skeletal (motor) nervous system that are spontaneously emitted without identifiable stimuli.

Objections and Rejoinders

This distinction has considerable appeal because evolution might reasonably be expected to have produced different methods of dealing with controllable and uncontrollable events. And, in fact, most research on classical conditioning aims to alter such behavior as the galvanic skin response, the salivary reflex, and cardiac reactions that are chiefly controlled by the autonomic nervous system; most research on instrumental conditioning involves motor responses like running a maze, pecking a key, or pressing a lever to obtain food or avoid punishment. But there is a body of research that calls the distinction into question. Experiments I describe below on autoshaping and biofeedback seem, respectively, to demonstrate the classical conditioning of skeletal responses and the instrumental conditioning of visceral reactions. Taken at face value, these results support the older view that there is only one kind of learning. If this idea is correct, the notion that the two procedures capture a distinction between adaptation and coping must be wrong.

Autoshaping: Classical Conditioning of Motor Responses?   In a typical autoshaping experiment, hungry pigeons receive a series of trials on
which the key in the standard key-pecking apparatus is illuminated
for a few seconds (CS), after which a hopper opens and the bird has
access to grain (US), which it pecks and eats (the unconditioned re-
sonse, UR). As in classical conditioning, the CS-US sequence happens
no matter what the pigeon does. But after several pairings of the
lighted key and food, the bird begins to peck at the key (conditioned
response, CR).

The conclusion that autoshaping is classical conditioning of skeletal
responses is not completely warranted, however. The key-pecking response in these experiments is based on hunger, which has important
autonomic components. It may be that these autonomic reactions are
conditioned in these experiments and they produce the instrumental
behavior that is natural for an animal of that species in that physiological condition. It may be that the instrumental responses are mediated
by autonomic reactions. That possibility (in reverse) is clearer in experiments on biofeedback.

Biofeedback: Operant Conditioning of Visceral Responses?   Biofeedback is
a method of informing people about the state of such visceral reactions
as heart rate, muscle tension, and blood pressure, of which they usually are unaware. Provided with such knowledge and the opportunity
to control them, people have learned with surprising ease to increase
or to decrease the levels of these responses. Such learning is not a
decisive demonstration of the instrumental conditionability of involuntary responses, however, because of the ease with which these responses can be mediated by voluntary instrumental activity. If
someone offered you a fortune to raise your heart rate on command,
you would quickly find an easy way to do so. In response to the command, you might jump up and down a few times to produce the de-
sired result. Even thinking about some form of exercise would be
enough.

Interpretation
As long as common speech remains its language, psychology must
strive to use that tool precisely. It is important, in this case, to recognize
that the terms *classical* and *instrumental conditioning* have two different meanings. Sometimes they refer to the *operations* (procedures)
employed in experiments with stimulus-stimulus or response-
consequence contingencies. At other times they refer to the *effects* of
those procedures. Autoshaping and biofeedback qualify as classical
and instrumental operations, but they fail to demonstrate that the ef-

fects obtained with these procedures are the same. A version of this same distinction, between procedures and outcomes, is important to the concept of emotion.

Categories of Affect

In 1960, O. Hobart Mowrer suggested that four different physical relationships between conditioned and unconditioned stimuli in classical conditioning provide operational definitions of four basic emotions. Mowrer introduced his thesis, as I began this chapter, with the observation that the unconditioned stimuli in classical conditioning are two different kinds of reinforcers: positive and negative. He then went on to note that conditioned stimuli occupy one of two positions with respect to a reinforcer: they may signify either its presence or imminent onset, or its absence or approaching termination. The possible combinations of two stimulus positions with two types of reinforcer define four emotions that Mowrer called *hope* (the CS predicts a positive reinforcer), *disappointment* (the CS predicts the absence of a positive reinforcer), *fear* (the CS predicts a negative reinforcer), and *relief* (the CS predicts the absence of a negative reinforcer). These four emotions provide a set of categories that can be extended to include a greater range of emotions by adding to the roster of defining operations those that distinguish between emotions produced by memories of past happenings and future expectations and those produced by one's own actions and environmental stimuli, including those provided by the behavior of other people.

The entries in table 4.1 are the names that ordinary speech might give to some of those additional emotions. What I call "pleasure" is the emotion that Mowrer called "hope." I used this different terminology because I needed the word "hope" for anticipated pleasure and relief. This distinction is typical of the problems that arise in any effort to use popular names for the emotions. Sometimes the best names I could think of for the emotions produced by different operations were the same. Beyond that, everyone will disagree with some of the names that I came up with. I frequently disagree myself.

These problems become less troublesome with a recognition, in this context, of the distinction between operations and effects that I made for classical and instrumental conditioning. Operations like those identified in table 4.1 give operational meaning to these concepts of emotion; the names they go by are of no significance. The important question is not what the effects of these different operations are called; it is their impact on behavior. Such responses as facial expression and differential physiology, if it exists, are two possibly important manifes-

Table 4.1
A Taxonomy of Emotion

The stimulus predicts	Type of reinforcer	
	Positive	Negative
Presence of reinforcer	*Primary Emotion*	
	Pleasure	Pain
	Oriented to the Past	
	Satisfaction	Resentment
	Oriented to the Future	
	Hope	Fear
	When the Stimuli are Environmental (Including other People)	
	Gratitude	Blame
	When the Stimuli are Self-Generated	
	Pride	Guilt
Absence of reinforcer	*Primary Emotion*	
	Disappointment	Relief
	Oriented to the Past	
	Regret	Safety
	Oriented to the Future	
	Apprehension	Hope
	When the Stimuli are Environmental (Including other People)	
	Mistrust	Gratitude
	When the Stimuli are Self-Generated	
	Remorse	Power

tations. Another is that in instrumental learning, emotions should serve the same purposes as positive and negative reinforcers, of which they are surrogates. A later section in this chapter, on two-process adjustments, will demonstrate the validity of that expectation.

Categories of Action

The discussion of the categories of behavior that occur in instrumental conditioning can be brief because the points are parallel to those that apply to the categories of emotion produced by classical conditioning. Whereas in classical conditioning, a CS may signify the presence or the absence of a positive or negative reinforcer, in instrumental conditioning a specified response may produce or prevent the occurrence of the same events. Possible combinations of these two consequences of responses and two types of reinforcer yield the instrumental-conditioning paradigms and the predicted outcomes presented in figure 4. 1. Until they are complicated by the considerations that we turn to next, these outcomes occur dependably.

Contingency and Causality

A more complete definition of the contingency between X and Y than the if "if X, then Y" statement requires the specification of two probabilities: the probability of Y, given X, and the probability of Y, given not-X; that is the probabilities that Y's occurring in the presence and absence of X. In classical conditioning, these probabilities are the probability of the US, given occurrence of the CS, and the probability of the US, given nonoccurrence of the CS. In instrumental conditioning, they are the probability of reinforcement, given the occurrence and nonoccurrence of a specified response.

The strengths of these contingencies may be defined as the probability of the US or reinforcer, given the CS or specified response, minus the probability of the US or reinforcer, given the absence of the CS or response. In classical conditioning, the strength of the contingency is an index of the *predictability* of the US; the instrumental contingency is an index of the *controllability* of a positive or negative reinforcer. The special cases in which the strength of the contingency is zero—Y is

		Type of Reinforcer	
		Positive	Negative
Effect of response on reinforcer	Produces	Reward training: Evokes action	Passive avoidance: Inhibits action
	Prevents	Omission training: Inhibits action	Active avoidance: Evokes action

Figure 4.1
Effects of Response-Reinforcer Contingencies
At the level of procedures, a specified response may produce or prevent a positive or negative reinforcer. Although there is some variation in the literature, these procedures often go by the names given first in each cell of the resulting contingency table. The effects of these two procedures on behavior are to evoke the specified response or to inhibit it, often by the activation of an incompatible reaction. Although the proposal is controversial, I believe that the logical designation of the procedures employed in reward training and active avoidance is positive reinforcement and that the logical designation for the procedures employed in omission training and passive avoidance is negative reinforcement (Kimble 1993).

equally probable given either the occurrence or the nonoccurrence of X—define unpredictability and uncontrollability for stimulus-stimulus and response-consequence contingencies, respectively.

Contingency Spaces

Figure 4.2 puts the probabilities for classical conditioning into a contingency space, a graphic way of showing how the CS-US relationship involves predictability. To the extent that the CS predicts the occurrence of the US, there is a positive contingency; to the extent that the absence of the CS predicts the US, there is a negative contingency. Figure 4.3 presents the contingency space for instrumental learning, where the response-outcome relationship involves controllability. Again, the space contains regions corresponding to positive and negative contingencies.

If learning matched the contingencies represented in these two graphs exactly, there would be excitatory conditioning when contingencies are positive and inhibitory conditioning when contingencies

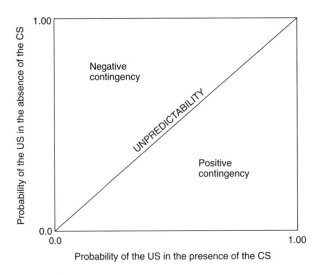

Probability of the US in the presence of the CS

Figure 4.2
Contingency Space in Classical Conditioning
A contingency space for classical conditioning is defined in terms of two probabilities: the probability of the occurrence of the US, given the occurrence (horizontal axis) or nonoccurrence (vertical axis) of the CS. Positive contingencies exist whenever the first of these two probabilities is greater than the second; negative contingencies exist whenever the second probability is greater. Positive contingencies lead to excitatory conditioning; negative contingencies lead to inhibitory conditioning. The absence of a contingency is the operational definition of unpredictability.

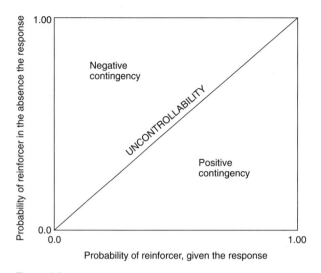

Figure 4.3
Contingency Space in Instrumental Conditioning
A contingency space for instrumental conditioning is defined in terms of two probabilities: the probability of the occurrence of a reinforcer, given the occurrence (horizontal
axis) or nonoccurrence (vertical axis) of a specified response. Positive contingencies exist
whenever the first of these two probabilities is greater than the second; negative contingencies exist whenever the second probability is greater. Positive contingencies exist in
reward training and active avoidance (figure 4.1). They lead to excitatory conditioning
and the strengthening of the reinforced reaction. Negative contingencies exist in omission training and passive avoidance. They lead to inhibitory conditioning and the inhibition of the specified response. The absence of a contingency is the operational definition
of uncontrollability.

are negative. The strength of these conditionings would vary directly
with the strength of the contingency. In the cases where no contingency
exists, there would be no conditioning at all. When the probabilities of
occurrence of a US or a reinforcer are those represented at the north-
west and southeast corners of the two contingency spaces, the predicted outcomes (inhibitory and excitatory classical conditioning, and
the four varieties of instrumental conditioning shown in figure 4.1)
actually occur. Other probabilities, which are much more common in
the real world, produce results of great consequence.

Unpredictability: Inability to Adapt and Impaired Affect   In a series of experiments with rats, Jay M. Weiss (1970) studied the stress produced
by predictable and unpredictable punishment. He used the size of
stomach ulcers in these animals as his main index of stress. There were
three groups of subjects in Weiss's experiments. One group received a

series of electric shocks, delivered through electrodes attached to their tails and preceded by a warning tone. A second, yoked-control, group received the same shocks as the first group but without the warning signal. The yoked-control animals were paired with (yoked to, "wired in parallel" with) a partner in the first group so that they received exactly the same shocks as their partner did. The difference was that the rats in the second group received no warning signal. A third, standard control group received no shock at all.

The animals in all of these three groups developed ulcers, indicating that all of the procedures produced some degree of stress. The evidence for the power of unpredictability was that the ulcers of the rats in the yoked-control group were some five times larger than those of the animals in the other groups. These findings probably apply to human beings. Although we tend to associate ulcers with coping, regarding it as a disease that occurs in hard-working, aggressive men, data collected over the years (Strang 1989) show that the individuals who are most at risk for this disorder are men who are particularly submissive and dependent. Ulcers are a symptom of inadequate adaptation rather than a sign of coping.

Uncontrollability: Inability to Cope and Impaired Reaction Tendency
Steven Maier and Martin Seligman (1976) studied the effect of controllable and uncontrollable electric shock in experiments with dogs, using a hurdle-jumping apparatus, whereby the animals could avoid electric shock by jumping a low barrier before the shock came on. Their ease of mastering that reaction depended on their experience with shock before the tests in the hurdle-jumping apparatus began. The plan of the experiment was similar to the design Weiss used in his studies of unpredictability. There were three groups of dogs in the experiment. Those in one group were strapped into an apparatus where they received shocks that they could terminate by turning their heads and pressing a panel. The dogs in the second groups were in a yoked-control condition; they received the same shocks as the animals in the first group but could not control the duration of the shocks. The animals in third, standard control, condition received no shock at all.

In a second stage of the experiment, the animals were tested in the hurdle-jumping apparatus. The dogs in the first and third groups learned the response quickly, but many of the animals in the yoked-control group failed to learn, even though their responses would now avoid the shock. The commonly accepted explanation for this effect is that animals previously given uncontrollable shock had learned that their responses had no effect on the environment; they were helpless.

Subsequent experiments—with unsolvable problems instead of electric shock—demonstrated that learned helplessness occurs in human beings as well. Dweck and Reppucci (1973) proposed that learned helplessness is one reason that some schoolchildren fail in mathematics. These youngsters are helpless because they see no relationship between their success in solving problems. They fail and experience punishment in the form of criticism and failure no matter what they do. Dweck and Repucci also showed that training children to persist in study instead of giving up produces improvements in their school performance.

Even more impressive, Ellen Langer and Judith Rodin (1976) demonstrated that helplessness can lower life expectancy. They gave two groups of patients in a nursing home a plant to tend and the opportunity to go to movies. One of these two groups cared for the plants themselves and chose when to see the movies. For the other group, patients on another floor, the nurses cared for the plants and took the patients to the movies at the same times as those in the first group—in effect, a yoked-control procedure. Observations a few weeks later indicated that the elderly patients who had this modest control over their existences were more active and had more positive moods than those in the comparison group. They also were healthier: a year later, fewer of them had died than the patients on the other floor (Rodin 1986).

The Perception of Causality and Its Distortions

The terms defining a contingency have much in common with those that designate causality. As close as I can come to a satisfactory definition of that elusive concept (p. 13) is that the cause of an event, Y, is another event, X, which has an if-and-only-if relationship Y: if X is present, then Y always occurs, and if X is absent, then Y never occurs. The everyday exposure of individuals to the "if X, then Y" half of this definition produces the perception of causality.

The potential for the perception of cause-effect relationships appears to be inborn. In experiments where a spot of light moves toward a second light and stops, and then the second light continues the movement in the same direction, Michotte (1963) has shown that people perceive the first motion as causing the second. His data also indicate that the perception of causality is direct, immediate, and unconscious rather than the product of logical analysis and inference. Piaget (1930) described behavior suggesting that the rudiments of this perception are present in children before the age of two. The consequences of this easy perception of causality are both positive and negative. They underlie the recognition of true cause-effect relationships, but they also lead people to see causality in situations where it does not exist.

Although it is common gossip that correlation does not prove causation, people are less aware that sometimes correlations do not even prove correlation. The perception of a stimulus-stimulus contingency when none exists is a "spurious correlation." The belief in response-outcome contingency when none exists is a "superstition." Spurious correlations and superstitions, respectively, are aberrations of adaptation and coping.

Spurious Correlations
In their philosophies of poker, many people hypothesize that a long series of bad or good hands increases the probability that the next hand will be the opposite (the gambler's fallacy) or, alternatively, "When you're hot, you're hot, and when you're not, you're not" (streak theory, or the good and bad hands will continue). At the poker table, and other situations where events occur at random, these spurious correlations do not exist.

The most important factor that keeps these fallacies alive is a tendency to put more faith in positive than in negative evidence. People remember happenings that support what they believe and discount negative instances, which "only prove the rule." In clinical practice, this tendency has encouraged the use of invalid methods of assessment like the Rorschach Inkblot Test.

In one study (Little and Schneidman 1959), twelve eminent Rorschach experts assessed the personalities of several psychiatric patients and compared their conclusions with the pooled judgments of a number of psychiatrists who diagnosed each patient. The mean correlation between the Rorschach expert's evaluations and the psychiatric diagnoses was a dismal +.21. Despite such evidence, projective techniques remain in widespread use in clinical practice, chiefly because of clinicians' impression that the correlation is stronger than it actually is. They remember the occasional successes and forget the vastly greater number of mistakes.

Superstitions
Something similar accounts for the survival of ineffective psychotherapeutic methods, like psychoanalysis. Clinicians have better memories for their cures than for their casualties. This faulty perception of clinical effectiveness is a superstition that is similar to the basketball coach's superstitious insistence on wearing his lucky tie at every game and players' crossing themselves before they attempt a free throw. They imagine cause-effect connections that do not exist.

Even lower animals can acquire such faulty understandings of cause-effect relationships. B. F. Skinner showed that pigeons developed "superstitions" in an experiment where grain appeared at fixed intervals in the food hopper of a standard Skinner pigeon box, no matter what the pigeons did. These superstitions consisted of complex chains of activity that occurred in the interval between deliveries of food: for example, circling the experimental compartment, bowing before the hopper as though it were an altar, and then waiting in apparent expectation that food would be forthcoming. Anthropomorphically, it was as though the pigeons believed that their ritualistic actions caused the delivery of this blessing.

Two-Process Adjustments

In the world of everyday existence, the contingencies for adaptation and coping exist together. Thus, in any situation, behavior is, in part, a function of the sequences of events that predictably occur there and, in part, a function of what the individual can do about them. With experience, the order of the individual's responses to these events becomes the Piagetian sequence: people respond to the signals of events in ways that increase or decrease their probabilities of occurrence. But the history of such adjustments is likely to be the opposite of this pattern. First, there is the classical conditioning of an emotional reaction (a form of adaptation) based on a stimulus-stimulus contingency. Then, second, this emotional reaction motivates and provides the basis for reward in the instrumental learning of coping responses.

Conditioned Positive Reinforcers and Token Rewards
Neutral stimuli associated with positive events acquire the power to elicit positive affective reactions; Mowrer would call these consequences "hope." Once established, such reactions become rewards. The potency of approval, money, and prestige attests to their effectiveness. The development of the rewarding power of such secondary reinforcers is difficult to trace in human beings because it is the result of a long and complicated history, but experiments with other animals suggest the essential features of that history.

Wolfe's (1936) study of token incentives with chimpanzees is a classical example. The tokens in this experiment were small disks, similar to poker chips, to which the animals originally were indifferent. Preliminary training, in which the chimpanzees learned the reward value of the tokens, consisted of training them to insert tokens into a vending apparatus that automatically released a grape, one of the animals' favorite foods. After this first phase of the experiment, the chimpanzees learned to perform instrumental responses, such as operating a lever or pulling in a tray attached to a string, to secure tokens. They mastered these tasks and continued to work at them, even though the tokens could not be exchanged for food until later on—as though they were hoarding them.

The token economies that are sometimes set up in mental institutions are large-scale applications of this same technique but using an already-established secondary reinforcer. Patients in these programs earn paper "currency" when they perform desirable behavior, such as cooperation, good manners, personal hygiene, or taking medicine. Later, these tokens can be redeemed for other reinforcers: special food, visits home, or even release from the hospital.

Conditioned Negative Reinforcers and Avoidance Learning
In parallel to what happens with positive events, neutral stimuli associated with negative events become negative secondary reinforcers; they strengthen behavior that removes them. The image of the dentist's office becomes aversive because of its association with pain, and you may learn better dental habits to avoid it.

In laboratory experiments with rats, such avoidance learning is sometimes studied with an apparatus that has an electrifiable grid as a floor and a sort of paddle wheel in one wall. A typical trial in such an experiment begins with the presentation of a warning signal (say, a light), which is followed in a few seconds by shock delivered to the floor. If the rat moves the paddle wheel after the shock comes on, that response turns it off. If it rotates the wheel during the interval between the signal and the shock, the shock does not come on.

On the first few trials of the experiment, before the rat has learned about the contingency between wheel turning and shock avoidance, it does not rotate the wheel and is shocked, in the presence of the light. The animal's reactions include various signs of fear: increased heart rate, defecation and urination, dilation of the peripheral blood vessels, squealing, jumping and clawing at the wheel and turning it. As the experiment proceeds, the rat makes this last response sooner and sooner, and after a few trials, it turns the wheel to the signal and avoids the shock completely.

In these experiments, rats learn two different things. One is that the initially uncontrollable light-shock contingency teaches it to fear the light (a classically conditioned emotional response). This conditioned fear functions as a motive. It energizes all of the reactions that the rat makes when it is afraid, and, in the process, the animal accidentally rotates the paddle wheel. The other is that the rat learns to turn the wheel immediately as a reaction to the light (an instrumentally conditioned motor reaction) because this action prevents delivery of the shock. With the occurrence of that response, the light goes off and the rat's fear subsides, providing a reward for wheel turning.

This simple learning process explains certain human psychopathological adjustments. In the obsessive-compulsive disorder, for example, classical conditioning establishes anxieties (obsessions) that people cannot drive from consciousness unless they perform certain actions (compulsions), which so occupy their attention there is no room for the obsessive ideas. Consider this example:

> Ms. A was a strikingly beautiful 23-year-old woman who came for psychotherapy because her obsessive fear that her heart would stop beating had led to the compulsive habit of counting her heartbeats. The compulsion was so powerful that it occupied her life and made other activities impossible. The origins of Ms. A's obsession were clear from her case history. Born an orphan, she had been brought up by a foster mother whose exceedingly repressive sex training made her feel that sex was evil and dirty. In spite of her upbringing, Ms. A developed an unusually strong sexual appetite, which led to fantasies that made her feel painfully guilty. Probably cardiac symptoms were associated with the guilt, suggesting the frightening idea that her heart would stop beating. The compulsion was Ms. A's way of dealing with this fear. Counting her heartbeats drove her fantasies and the attendant guilt out of consciousness, making life livable but worthless. (Dollard and Miller 1950)

The symptoms of obsessive-compulsive disorder have the same accidental quality as the wheel turning of the rat. In Ms. A's case, many other responses might have served the same protective purpose, including the avoidance of the number 13. In one classical case (Ross 1937), the patient was a forty-nine-year-old man who experienced intense anxiety whenever he heard or saw the number thirteen. It seemed as though everyone was always saying "thirteen" at him. In the morning, it was "Oh, good morning"; later in the day, it was "Good afternoon"—thirteen letters in each greeting. He stayed in bed on the thirteenth day of every month, skipped the thirteenth tread in a stairway, and counted letters, his footsteps, and streets in order to avoid thirteen. This neurosis, as with Ms. A's, dates back to a time in adolescence when he was living with a very religious grandmother. He managed to elude her supervision from time to time and over a period of two years had a sexual affair with a household servant who was suspicious about thirteen. Feeling very much ashamed of his behavior, he adopted this superstition himself. In obsessive-compulsive adjustments, the response, whatever it happens to be, is a way of coping with intense feelings of fear, guilt, or anxiety.

This explanation of the origins of the obsessive-compulsive symptoms resolves what was called the neurotic paradox in the days before psychology gave up the useful word "neurosis." Neurotic behavior is paradoxical because it is stupidly persistent, given that it seems to bring the patient nothing but misery. The paradox disappears with the recognition that the symptoms bring an important form of reward: relief from anxiety and fear.

Adaptation and Coping in Other Contexts

Varieties of adaptation and coping appear across the entire spectrum of topics in psychology. Coping is behavior that is active, constructive, and dynamic; adaptation is behavior that is passive, reproductive, and static. Much of the content of this chapter derives from the fact that classical conditioning is adaptation and instrumental conditioning is coping. Extensions of this conception give meaning to the distinction between helplessness and competence, as well as to the neurotic adjustments of obsession and compulsion.

Elsewhere, as the terms "sensation" and "perception" are usually defined, sensation is a set of largely passive, bottom-up (adaptive) mechanisms that register the attributes of stimulation somewhere in the nervous system; perception is the product that more active, top-down (coping) mechanisms create from those materials. Although coping is often voluntary, deliberate, and conscious, it need not be. The constructive processes that make perceptions out of sensory information are involuntary and automatic. They are what Helmholtz called *unconscious inference.*

Within-Individual Differences

The mechanisms of adaptation and coping are available to everyone, for uses that depend on situations. They appear in all of Aristotle's knowing-feeling-doing categories. In cognition, the examples of adaptation include recognition (passive memory), passive vocabulary (the words you know), and receptive aphasia (lost language comprehension)—an inability to adapt. Coping includes recall (constructive memory), active vocabulary (the words you use), and expressive aphasia (loss of verbal expression)—an inability to cope. In the world of affect, adaptation is extrinsic (environmental) motivation; coping is intrinsic motivation (motivation from within). For reaction tendencies, adaptation is automatic, thoughtless, involuntary, reflexive behavior; coping is deliberate, thoughtful, voluntary problem-solving action.

Between-Individual Differences

The distinction between adaptation and coping also defines some of the ways in which individuals differ in their habitual reactions to the world. In the case of reasoning, for example, Hanfmann and Kasanin (1937) noted long ago that people used different strategies to solve a problem that required them to sort blocks differing in shape, size, and color into groups that had certain arbitrary nonsense names. Although they were allowed to manipulate the blocks and inspect the names in their attempts to solve the problem, some subjects employed a passively inactive strategy; they simply sat and looked at the blocks, waiting for solutions to come to mind spontaneously. Others used a conceiving strategy; they formed hypotheses about the solution and tested these hypotheses by checking the category names. The distinction here is the perceiving (adapting)/judging (coping) dimension of personality on the Myers-Briggs Type Inventory, which is a much better validated instrument than is commonly believed (Myers 1962).

In another much-studied example, some people are "field dependent" ("field oriented"). They have "external locus of control" and think that outside forces—chance, luck, the physical environment, and other people—are in command of their behavior. Others are "body oriented" ("field independent"). They have "internal locus of control" and think that their behavior is determined by their personal dispositions—effort, ability, motivation, and stick-to-itiveness. For people with external locus of control, the most important values are fame, attractiveness, and material possessions. For people with internal locus of control, they are friendships, creativity, and personal growth.

Summary and Conclusions

The adjustments of organisms in the world today are the evolutionary consequence of a struggle to obtain and to avoid what psychology calls positive and negative reinforcers: the "good" things required for nurturance and continuation of the species, and the "bad" things that threaten security. Behavior is a blend of two mechanisms that further these objectives: coping, when control over the environment is possible, and adaptation, when it is not. When organisms are coping, they remain what they were and adjust by doing things that change the world. When they adapt, they change themselves, in order to survive in an unyielding environment.

The science of psychology expresses these relationships as contingencies: the joint probabilities that a reinforcer will or will not occur in the presence or the absence of specific stimuli or responses. Classical and operant conditioning are laboratory analogues of these stimulus-

stimulus and response-outcome contingencies. Respectively, they represent the operations that lead to adaptation and coping. It appears that these two procedures operate on different categories of behavior. Classical conditioning modifies involuntary responses of the autonomic nervous system. Instrumental conditioning modifies voluntary responses of the skeletal nervous system.

In a related way of thinking, stimulus-reinforcer contingencies define predictability; response-reinforcer contingencies define controllability. When predictability and control are perfect, organisms behave appropriately. When these contingencies are less than perfect, they often behave as though they were able to predict events and control them better than they actually can. They see (spurious) correlations between events where none exists and develop superstitions that provide them with an unrealistic impression of control.

Outside the laboratory, behavior is a combination of coping and adaptation. The history of such practical adjustments is one in which signals of events to which adaptation is the only possible reactions provide the warnings that the organism needs to achieve appropriate coping. This learning is the origin of foresight, which allows the organism to anticipate significant events and take actions that increase or decrease the probability of those happenings.

Such experience provides everyone with the abilities to cope in certain situations and to adapt in others, but some people develop better coping skills, and others depend more on adaptation. The result is the contrasting personal styles of people with external or internal locus of control and extrinsic or intrinsic motivation.

Chapter 5

Opponent-Process Theory

The notion that behavior is under the simultaneous control of rival forces appeared in Aristotle's writings. Even earlier, prior to the sixth century B.C., the Asian cosmologies took the interactions of yin and yang to be responsible for every phenomenon of nature. Yin was earth, female, dark, passive, and absorbing. It was present in even numbers, valleys, and streams and was represented by the color orange, the tiger, and broken lines. Yang was heaven, male, light, active, and penetrating. It was present in odd numbers and mountains and represented by the color azure, the dragon, and unbroken lines. The parallels to Freudian dream symbolism suggest that the similarities are not accidental. Yin and yang are constantly in conflict; when one increases, the other decreases. Lasting harmony is achieved when the two are balanced.

In 1686, Sir Isaac Newton advanced the idea that opposing forces control physical phenomena. In his third law of motion, he hypothesized, "To every action there is always opposed an equal reaction: or, the mutual reactions of two bodies upon each other are always equal, and directed to contrary parts" (Cajori 1947, p. 13).

In more modern times, William James recognized the existence of conflicting influences on behavior and acknowledged their importance. He noted that *"nature implants contrary impulses to act on many classes of things"* (James 1890a, 2:392). In many contexts, one of the conflicting processes is inhibition, which James gave the same causal status as he assigned to activation: "Inhibition is a *vera causa*, of that there can be no doubt" (1:67). He also recognized that inhibition operates in mental as well as physical activities, as is demonstrated by the phenomenon of satiated meaning: "If [you] look at an isolated printed word and repeat it long enough . . . it stares at [you] from the paper like a glass eye, with no speculation in it" (1:81).

A Neurophysiological Process with Connections to Behavior

Communication among the neurons is a chemical conversation. When impulses reach their terminal buttons, presynaptic neurons release small packets of a neurotransmitter that crosses a synapse, transferring information to adjacent cells. When these signals produce a reaction in a postsynaptic neuron, they are excitatory. When they reduce the likelihood of a reaction, they are inhibitory. Target neurons receive inputs from many presynaptic neurons—some excitatory, some inhibitory. How they respond depends on the balance among these signals.

A Selection of Examples

Synaptic transmission appears to set a basic pattern for behavior. Interactions between excitation and inhibition occur in contexts that cover the entire spectrum of psychological adjustments.

Sensory Processes and Perception   Color vision is the result of interactions among the outputs of three types of cones that may have excitatory or inhibitory consequences in the thalamus, depending on the cells with which they are connected. Shape perception depends on the detection of edges and contours that result from the mutual inhibition of adjacent cells in the retina. Elsewhere in the sensory world, pain registers its presence via a system that may enhance or dampen that experience. The same system also sharpens or dulls attention.

The neurophysiology of pain is fairly well understood. Aversive stimulation causes the hypothalamus to release a cortico-releasing factor (CRF), which signals the pituitary to release ACTH (adrenocorticotrophic hormone) and opioids, including the endorphins ("endogenous morphine"). ACTH and the endorphins have opposite effects: ACTH heightens pain, and the endorphins diminish it. These mechanisms appear to be the prototype of how we handle pain of all sorts, including the mental pain produced by stress and trauma, probably because stress and pain so often occur together: "In nature, pain comes delivered in an envelope of stress" (Goleman 1985, p. 31). Thus, it is to be expected that purely psychological stress will trigger the same mechanisms as noxious physical stimulation.

Attention   The neurophysiology of pain is closely tied to the processes that control attention: ACTH enhances it, and the endorphins diminish it. In attention, excitation admits and inhibition excludes relevant and irrelevant inputs from consciousness. Afferent signals may be blocked, so that unimportant information does not reach the brain at all. In an experiment that became a classic, Hernandez-Peon, Scherer, and Jouvet (1956) studied the neurological responses of the cat to auditory stimuli, with the aid of electrodes implanted in the cochlear nucleus. The normal reaction of the brain to the presentation of a click was a large, evoked potential, but when the click was delivered simultaneously with the presentation of two mice in a glass jar, the neural response very nearly disappeared. Later studies suggested that this suppression is the result of impulses coming from higher levels of the nervous system, a conclusion that fits a general pattern of cognitive inhibition, discussed later in this chapter.

Similar happenings occur in human experience. Think of a cocktail party or some other noisy gathering where there are several conversations going on around you simultaneously. Attention to the one of greatest interest usually makes it easy to ignore the others. Nevertheless, the excluded conversations are still there in some sense. If talk in one of them turns to a topic of importance to you—for example, if someone drops your name—you are likely to redirect awareness and bring that conversation into focus.

Reflex Action   In the course of his work on spinal reflexes, the great neurophysiologist Sir Charles Sherrington (1857–1952) had the insight that the entire nervous system operates on the basis of a system of checks and balances involving excitation and inhibition. For example, the patellar reflex could not occur if some muscles were not inhibited at the same time as opposing muscles are excited (Sherrington 1906).

Conditioning and Complex Learning   As we saw in chapter 3 in the discussion of potentials and instigation, the processes of excitation and inhibition figure prominently in conditioning and higher learning. In conditioning, interactions between excitation and inhibition explain spontaneous recovery; in verbal and motor learning, they account for the negative effects of massed practice and reminiscence. All of these phenomena are increases in performance that occur after a brief rest that releases them from an inhibitory process.

Affect   In the realm of affect, the hunger motive is governed by excitatory and inhibitory processes with separate loci in the hypothalamus. In ethology, the theory of innate releasing mechanisms holds that an instinctive act appears when stimulation removes the inhibitory block that inhibits its expression. In situations where their lives are threatened, animals sometimes freeze when the opposite reaction, flight, would take them out of danger.

Imprinting   There is a tendency for the newborn infants of many species, particularly precocial birds, to follow the first large moving object that they see. This phenomenon, called *imprinting*, occurs most readily in a critical period that is determined by an interaction between tendencies to follow (an excitatory process) and to flee from (an opponent process) novel objects. Both tendencies increase with age, but avoidance increases faster and achieves a greater strength. The critical period for imprinting is the point at which the difference in favor of following between these two curves is maximal.

William James described these phenomena as though they were well known in 1890. He quoted D. A. Spalding who had reported in 1873 that if baby chicks are born in an incubator, they "will follow any moving object. And, when guided by sight alone, they seem to have no more disposition to follow a hen than a duck or a human being. Unreflecting onlookers, when they saw chickens a day old running after me for miles, and answering to my whistle, imagined that I must have some occult power over the creatures; whereas I had simply allowed them to follow me from the first." Spalding also knew that imprinting occurs only during a critical period early in the life of the chick. If such experience were postponed until later, the initial reaction would have been not following but fear (James 1890a, 2:396–398).

Adaptive Value
The interactions just considered are adaptive because in all of them, one process—either excitation or inhibition—promotes behavior with survival value and the other excludes behavior that is maladaptive. The dual control of behavior also has the useful power of keeping acts from going on forever. Although William James could not have known about Sherrington's work on reflexes, he understood the adaptive value of an arrangement that pitted inhibition against excitation: "We should all be cataleptics and never stop a muscular contraction once begun, were it not that other processes simultaneously going on inhibit the contraction (James 1890a, 2:583).

Sensation and Attention   The sharpening of attention that occurs as the first effect of noxious stimulation alerts the organism to present dangers and sets the stage for coping. The lessening of pain that follows is adaptive when coping mechanisms fail so that the organism must endure pain-producing stimulation. The functional value of the cocktail party phenomenon in attention is that it allows people to select for further processing the most important of the stimuli with which they are bombarded and eliminate the rest. Imagine the cluttered consciousness that we would have if that were not the case. Presumably the freezing of animals in danger occurs because they are harder for predators to see when they are absolutely still. This observation serves as a reminder that adaptive value is "on the average." Sometimes, for an individual, the outcome is the opposite of survival.

Conditioning   Pavlov recognized the adaptive usefulness of classical conditioning, but the major credit for bringing this understanding to the Western world goes to C. L. Hull. In 1929, Hull (then at the University of Wisconsin, later at Yale University) published a landmark paper, "A Functional Interpretation of the Conditioned Reflex," which showed that the major phenomena of conditioning are adaptive. Conditioned reflexes (excitation) allow an organism to anticipate the threats and opportunities that are signaled by conditioned stimuli and to deal with them appropriately. Conditioned salivation improves the taste of food; the conditioned blink protects the eye from irritation. Extinction (inhibition) brings such behavior to an end when signals become irrelevant. Stimulus generalization (of both excitation and inhibition) leads organisms to respond or not respond to classes of situations rather than to isolated stimuli. Discrimination, resulting from the inhibition of generalized reactions, confines the conditioned responses of the organism to situations where they are adaptive.

Later evidence demonstrated that the conditioning of inhibition is adaptive in an unexpected way. Such conditioning accounts for the developing tolerance of people addicted to a drug. The value of this inhibitory conditioning is that it protects the addict from possibly lethal (excitatory) consequences of an overdose. Siegel (1979, 1984) provided tragic evidence for this interpretation, with data showing that deaths from overdoses are more common when addicts take the drugs in unfamiliar situations—situations without the stimuli that evoke protective conditioned inhibition.

Imprinting   Imprinting is adaptive because it provides the basis for filial attachment. The most salient object in the first hours of an organism's existence is usually another member of its species, most often its mother, and the infant is imprinted on an agent of protection. Imprinting guarantees that infants will follow their mothers; when the mother flees from dangers such as predators, the young will quickly follow her to safety and survival. The tendency to flee prevents the extension of the infant's tendency to follow to potentially threatening objects.

Four Principles and One Proviso

Over the years, research on excitation and inhibition has yielded data to suggest that four major principles control the operation of these processes. The same history has also shown that the complexities surrounding the operation of these principles require the statement of a proviso.

First Principle   As Newton's third law suggests, excitation and inhibition are inseparable realities. Stimulation initiates both excitatory and inhibitory processes. The two processes are slaves to one another: excitation elicits inhibition, and inhibition elicits excitation.

Second Principle   The arithmetic of subtraction describes the interaction between the two: inhibition lessens excitation, and vice versa.

Third Principle   Excitation operates more rapidly than inhibition. As we saw in the case of pain, ACTH enhancement occurs before the numbing of that experience by the endorphins. ACTH and the endorphins are split off from the same master molecule. They are parts of a single neurochemical package, but ACTH affects the body within half a minute; the endorphins require something like two minutes.

Fourth Principle   Excitation and inhibition both persist for some time beyond the termination of the stimuli that produce them.

Proviso   In what may be a departure from the Newtonian idea, the strengths of the two processes may not be equal. Both the absolute and the relative strengths of excitation and inhibition depend on the details of situations. As William James put it, "[Nature] leaves it to slight alterations in the conditions of the individual case to decide which impulse shall carry the day" (James 1890a, 2:392). The quality that dominates depends upon contextual variables, including some within the individual, some in the environmental circumstances of the moment, and some that are the result of past learning.

Opponent-Processes in Action

In the following sections, I discuss the operation of these principles in the familiar contexts of cognition, affect, and reaction tendency, with the aid of evidence on visual afterimages, the time course of the emotions, and the phenomena of classical conditioning.

Opponent-Process Theory of Color Vision

In 1957, Leo Hurvich and Dorothea Jamieson described an opponent-process theory of color vision, a modernization of a theory developed in the 1870s by Ewald Hering (1834–1918). This theory maintains that the four psychologically primary colors—red, green, yellow, and blue—represent just two physiological processes—red-green and yellow-blue—in which the activation of one component (red or yellow) inhibits the other (green or blue). Hering had noticed that although most colors blend in our experience, certain colors cancel one another. Thus, red combines with yellow to produce orange, or with blue to produce violet, but a mixture of red and green or blue and yellow lights is colorless. Hering hypothesized that this happens because the red-green and yellow-blue processes can be activated in one direction only: to signal red or yellow, or in the opposite direction to signal green or blue. They cannot respond in both directions simultaneously because the response that corresponds to red inhibits the response for green, and the same relationship holds for blue and yellow. Each of the opponent processes subtracts from the other, and when the two are equal, the result is zero.

Opponent-process theory explains many of the facts of color vision, including negative afterimages. When a red light comes on in a semidarkened room, it produces an experience of redness that gains strength so rapidly that special experiments are required to trace the increase. If the light stays on, the experience of red remains but gradually loses some of its intensity. When the red light goes off, the redness persists momentarily as a positive afterimage, but soon it disappears, to be replaced by a green negative afterimage. The afterimage reaches its maximum intensity more slowly than the original experience had, and then it also fades away. These phenomena illustrate the four major principles and the proviso.

First, a red light turns on not just the processes that translate into that color but (a moment later) also the inhibitory "slave reaction" corresponding to the perception of the opponent color, green, which increases in strength with time. When the red light goes off, the green process becomes dominant, and what the observer sees is green. The green soon disappears, however, because the "slave process" for green is red, which cancels out the sense of green.

Second, the inhibitory process subtracts from the excitatory process, more and more as time goes on. Thus, as long as the red stimulus is there, what one experiences is chiefly red, but the sense of redness gradually loses strength because of the green opponent process.

Third, because the excitatory process is more rapid than the inhibitory process, the experience of red is almost immediate, when the red light comes on. The dimming of that experience happens later. After the red light goes off, the appearance of the afterimage takes time to develop; it happens less immediately than the experience of red.

Fourth, both of these processes persist following the termination of the stimulus that produced them—hence the positive afterimage after the red light goes off. After that, what one sees is chiefly a green negative afterimage that gains strength as the red mechanism dies away.

Proviso, the quality of the primary experience and the afterimage both depend on the intensity and duration of the red light, on the steadiness of the observer's fixation, on the color of the background against which the afterimage is projected, and on the distance of that background from the observer. Afterimages are also different for colorblind and normally sighted people.

Opponent-Processes Theory of Emotion
Although it is slower, the time course of emotional reactions parallels
the one described for negative afterimages. Without making that connection, Ivan Michailovich Sechenov (1829–1905), an approximate contemporary of Darwin, described the pattern (Sechenov 1935). He noted
that while emotions are strengthened and directed by continued practice, they are also subject to a second law of repetition. Repeated elicitation of an emotional reaction leads to its dulling and disappearance.
The only means of maintaining the strength of an emotion is through
the experience of constant change. The child grows weary of familiar
toys, and by exactly the same process, after two or three years of mar-
riage, the man and woman find that their passion has subsided
(sources of possible variation being now exhausted) and replaced by a
gentler, longer-lasting emotion.

Citing classical sources, William James made similar observations
about sequences of emotions. He agreed with Homer who had said
that "griefs are often afterwards of entertainment" (James 1890a, 2:550)
and Dante, who remarked "that the memory of griefs when past may
be a joy, and there is no greater sorrow than, in misery, to recollect
one's happier time" (1:497).

Solomon and Corbit (1973) developed a more formal opponent-
process theory to account for this pattern of emotional responses, beginning their presentation with the following example. In the hours
that follow her physician's report that she has breast cancer, a woman's
fear quickly rises to a maximum, but then decreases slightly. When
she learns later that the report was in error, her response (after she has
had the time to assimilate the good news) is not emotional grayness
but euphoria.

The basic principles in Solomon and Corbit's theory are the same as
those in the opponent-process theory of afterimages.

First Principle, an emotional event such as hearing the doctor's diagnosis of breast cancer (corresponding to the red light in the visual example) initiates a *state A* (fear) and also an opponent emotional
process, *state B* (euphoria). As in color vision state B is the slave of the
initial state A.

Second, emotional experience is the net result of the subtractive interaction of these two states.

Third, state A quickly rises to a peak; state B is slower.

Fourth, both processes persist in time. Although it loses some of its
intensity because of the damping influence of state B, state A remains
high as long as the emotional stimulus is present. When that stimulus
comes to an end (just as when the red light goes off), the original emo-

tional reaction subsides, giving way to its opposite state B—euphoria in the same example.

Proviso, the relative strengths of states A and B depend on other factors, of which one of the most important is frequency of emotional arousal. State B becomes stronger with practice, but state A does not, so that after many experiences of the same emotion, state B is more powerful than state A. These later reactions are so different that it will be useful to use the terms state A_1 and state A_2, to refer to those states early and later on, and to use state B_1 and state B_2 for the corresponding emotional aftermaths.

To illustrate the operation of the model, with the implications of this proviso included, let us consider two examples. The first is that of a dog that receives an unavoidable electric shock, in a conditioning experiment. During the first few shocks, the dog yelps and thrashes about, with its tail curled between its legs. Its hair stands on end, its eyes bulge, and the pupils dilate. Anthropomorphically, its emotional state A_1 is terror. When the dog is released from the harness, it is unfriendly, hesitant, and stealthy (state B_1). That reaction disappears within a few minutes, and the dog returns to its usual state.

After many exposures to this treatment, the dog's behavior becomes dramatically different. Now when shock comes on, the dog whines rather than yelps. Instead of looking terrorized, its state A_1 reaction, it looks pained, anxious, and annoyed. Away from the experiment, it jumps about, wags its tail, jumps up on people, and behaves as though it were in a fit of joy. This state B_2 is also very different from the earlier state B_1.

The second example comes from observations of sports parachutists. When parachutists are making their first few jumps, photos of their faces and measures of the responses of the autonomic nervous system reveal that state A_1 involves a look of terror and that their sympathetic nervous system is aroused. After they have landed safely, they appear stunned, stony-faced, and quiet (state B_1). After many jumps, the behavioral sequence is dramatically different. In state A_2, the parachutists are tense and expectant but no longer terrified. After landing, they are talkative and report that they feel exhilarated and jubilant (state B_2).

Opponent Processes in Conditioning

Pavlov thought of excitation and inhibition as dynamic processes, located in the cerebral hemispheres. Although he regarded them as separate entities, he considered excitation and inhibition to be intimately related. Sometimes he referred to them as the Greek god Janus, whose two faces look simultaneously in opposite directions. Although he did not refer to them in these terms, Pavlov's view of conditioning recognized the regularities of opponent-process functioning.

First Principle, the Janus metaphor implies the slave relationship between excitation and inhibition. Pavlov expressed that idea more technically in the concept of mutual induction: either excitation or inhibition induces (leaves in its wake) the opposite process. Thus, immediately following their arousal by the presentation during acquisition of a CS and reinforcement, the neural centers corresponding to the CS are inhibited, and immediately following the presentation of the CS without reinforcement in extinction, the same neural centers are excited.

Second, a basic assumption in Pavlovian theory was that excitation and inhibition subtract from each other. Excitation is a brain state that tends to evoke reflexes; inhibition is a state that works to restrain them. Pavlov hypothesized the existence of two different types of inhibition. *External inhibition* referred to the disruptive influences of extraneous stimulation, on either excitation or inhibition. *Internal inhibition* was conditioned inhibition, which develops whenever a CS is presented without a US, most obviously in extinction. Internal inhibition also occurs in discrimination learning, whenever the negative (unreinforced) stimulus is presented; in backward conditioning, where the US precedes the CS; and in the interval between the CS and US, where the presentation of a CS activates the CR, but also a form of inhibition called *inhibition of delay,* because the US is not immediately forthcoming. The external inhibition produced by a distracting stimulus can inhibit an established conditioned reflex, but it can also *disinhibit* reactions that are suppressed by inhibition of delay or abolished by extinction.

Third, the phenomenon of disinhibition is consistent with the idea that excitation is more rapid than inhibition. Although the animal does not respond during the early part of the interval between CS and US because of internal inhibition, the release of the conditioned reflex by disinhibition (external inhibition of inhibition) is evidence that the CR was previously there.

Fourth, the phenomena of long-interval trace conditioning show that excitatory processes persist in time. In such conditioning, the CS appears and disappears some time before the delivery of the US. The fact that conditioning occurs means that the excitatory process initiated by the CS continues to operate throughout the CS-US interval. In such long-interval conditioning, inhibition of delay also develops and persists, even to the time of delivery of the US, and the magnitude of the UR may be inhibited, in both dogs (Konorski 1948) and human beings (Kimble and Ost 1961).

Proviso, Pavlov's view of this interaction was more complex than those of the other opponent-process theorists considered in this section. In addition to the hypotheses of two forms of inhibition and mutual induction, Pavlovian theory maintained that the neural activities that correspond to excitation and inhibition first irradiate and then concentrate in the cerebral hemispheres. As a result, both processes first lose and then regain strength in time.

Another complicating factor was that the details of the interaction between excitation and inhibition depended on CS intensity. Increasing the strength of the CS increased the strength of excitation—up to the "top capability" of the cortical cells. At that point, induction reversed the process, and stronger stimulation became increasingly inhibitory.

Finally, Pavlov assigned great importance to individual differences in the strength and lability of excitation and inhibition, a point returned to later in this chapter.

Cognitive Inhibition

One of the most important factors in the collection of context variables included in the proviso ending each discussion in the section just completed is cognition. A major influence of cognition is to be inhibitory: it modulates behavior and wards off maladaptive actions.

A Glance at History

I. M. Sechenov proposed such a theory over a century ago. Entertaining the not-unreasonable hypothesis that the main function of the cerebral hemispheres is the management of intellectual activity, he had this to say: "When the impression [effect of a stimulus] is absolutely unexpected the reflex movement is effected exclusively through the nerve centre connecting sensory and motor nerves. But if the stimulation is expected, a new mechanism interferes with the phenomenon seeking to suppress and inhibit the reflex movement" (Sechenov 1935, p. 43).

Sechenov illustrated the inhibitory influence of cognition, as he often did, with the aid of an informal example. Suppose, with her consent, that you perform the following experiment on a nervous lady: Warning her that you are about to do so, you knock sharply on the table with your fist. Although she is prepared, she starts at the sharp sound. Continued knockings at the same intensity lead to the complete habituation of this reaction. Now, and again warning her of your intention, you increase the intensity of the sound. Again the nervous lady starts, and again continued knockings lead to habituation.

This demonstration reveals a basic principle of action. Unexpected stimuli evoke the reflex—nothing more—but expected stimuli also initiate an inhibitory process. Such inhibition is a function of the cerebral cortex. The results of your experiment would have been different had they been obtained following decortication of the nervous lady. Then her reflexes would have been machine-like, with a constant magnitude and not subject to habituation.

In support of essentially the same hypothesis, William James took note of data obtained by a Dr. Lombard, who found that intellectual effort raised the temperature on the scalp in human beings, and, "Strange to say, it was greater in reciting poetry silently than in reciting it aloud, [suggesting] if we must have a theory, that the surplus heat in recitation to one's self [more in the realm of thinking] is due to inhibitory processes which are absent when we recite aloud" (James 1890a, 1:100).

Generalities: The Range of Application

Several lines of more recent evidence also reveal that the higher levels of the central nervous system exercise an inhibitory influence on behavior. The spinal reflexes of paraplegic patients are abnormally strong, indicating that when their spinal cords were severed, these patients lost an inhibitory influence that had been provided by the higher levels of the central nervous system. Jerzy Konorski (1960) observed that following decortication, hungry dogs eat for longer than before the operation and the unconditioned salivary reflex is stronger. Jerome Bruner reports that stimuli that attract infants' attention interfere with one of their most important activities, sucking, and babies go to extremes to exclude distractions—at such an early age that learning seems unlikely to have much to do with the process: "At birth and for some days after, the infant sucks with the eyes tight shut. If the infant looks, tracks, or listens, sucking is disrupted.... With the [slightly older] three- to-five-week-old baby, the eyes may be open while sucking, but there is a high likelihood that when fixation or tracking occurs, sucking stops" (Bruner 1968, p. 18).

Specifics: Cognitive Inhibition in Classical Eyelid Conditioning

Experiments on human eyelid conditioning have become such a rarity that I will describe procedures so that the following example is understandable. Participants in these studies sit in a sound-deadened room, wearing head gear that carries two essential pieces of equipment: a tube and nozzle through which a puff of air can be delivered to the cornea to make the subject blink, and a microtorque potentiometer that tracks the subject's responses. One end of a length of thread is fastened to the arm of the potentiometer; the other is taped to the subject's eyelid, so that the arm of the potentiometer moves when the subject's eyelid moves. Fed through appropriate equipment, this system provides an ink-written record of the subject's responses.

On each of several tens of trials in an eyelid conditioning experiment, the sequence of events is as follows: A signal warning the participant that a trial is about to start may or may not be used. Whether one is used or not, the trials consist of pairings of a CS, which might be a small, dim light or a soft tone, and a US, usually an air puff. The interval between the CS and the US is brief—between a fraction of a second and a second and a half or so. In the early trials of such an experiment, subjects produce a blink only as a UR to the air puff; after a few trials, they begin to blink in response to the CS, before the US comes on. The frequency of such CRs increases with practice, up to a limit that depends on such variables as the interval between CS and US and US intensity.

Those of us who conducted such experiments forty years ago assumed that we were discovering the laws of classical conditioning. But in the end it became clear (at least to me) that the outcomes of these experiments had more to do with the cognitions of the subjects than they did with the process of conditioning.

Two kinds of learning take place in an eyelid conditioning experiment. The first is *cognitive learning,* the acquisition of knowledge of what happens in the experiment: such things as the significance of the ready signal if there is one, the patterning of reinforced and nonreinforced trials in an experiment that employs a partial schedule, and the fact that reinforcement follows one stimulus and not another in a discrimination learning experiment. The second is *classical conditioning,* the establishment of the conditioned blink. Subjects' descriptions provide operational validity for this distinction. Questioning reveals that cognitive learning occurs in subjects who never produce a CR throughout an experiment. The increasing frequency of CRs is the evidence for conditioning.

Cognitive learning happens in the first few trials of a conditioning experiment. During these early trials, the learning curves obtained with procedures that promote (even minor) cognitive involvement fall below the curves obtained without them. The separation of such functions occurs almost immediately, and the two curves remain separated throughout the experiment. I have described this outcome for a variety of experiments in which the procedures lend themselves to cognitive understanding: the use of ready signals, partial reinforcement, and discrimination learning (Kimble 1971, pp. 76–81).

Individual Differences

Pavlov (1927) was impressed with the differences he observed in the "temperaments" of his experimental subjects. Some, he said, were "positively indifferent" and poor subjects; it was necessary to use "impressionable and excitable" animals for success in the experiment. Later he developed these ideas into a theory of types of nervous system. He proposed that animals vary on three fundamental dimensions: (1) the absolute strengths of the basic processes of excitation and inhibition, (2) the relative balance between these two processes, and (3) the lability of excitation and inhibition in an individual nervous system.

These three dimensions provide for great variety in temperament if one assumes there are many possible positions for an animal to occupy on each dimension and that positions on dimensions are uncorrelated. In practice, however, Pavlov tended to posit four types of temperament, corresponding to those identified by Hippocrates (ca. 460–377 B.C.): melancholic, choleric, phlegmatic, and sanguine.

The melancholic temperament was weak in both excitatory and inhibitory processes—so weak that the dimensions of balance and mobility were unimportant. Conditioned responses in these dogs were difficult to establish and easily disrupted by distracting stimulation. Outside the laboratory, they were vulnerable to breakdown under stressful conditions.

The choleric dog was strong but unequilibrated, excitation being dominant. It developed positive CRs with ease but negative CRs with difficulty. Outside the laboratory, it might be aggressive and emotional or depressed.

Phlegmatic animals were strong and equilibrated. Both positive and negative CRs are easy to establish, and they remained stable once established. Outside the laboratory these animals were generally calm, although they had difficulty in responding to changed environmental conditions.

Sanguine animals were strong and equilibrated. With adequate stimulation, they were easily conditionable. With less than adequate stimulation, they tended toward drowsiness and sleep. Outside the laboratory, their external behavior was buoyant and energetic.

Pavlov suspected that the behavioral differences observed outside the laboratory reflected differences on the third dimension, mobility. He regarded this as an important matter for future investigation and theoretical development.

Applications to Human Personality

Over the years, psychologists have advanced a succession of accounts of individual differences in human personality that bear a clear relationship to the Pavlovian typology (Zuckerman 1991). In one way or another, excitation and inhibition are central to these theories, and these concepts are the major sources of variation in some of them. They classify individuals on such dimensions as extroversion-introversion, excitability-inhibitability, sensitization-repression, and impulsivity–self-control. As Pavlov would have anticipated, there is good evidence that variance on these dimensions has a strong component of heritability.

The reactions that people make to stress provide a collection of examples of the opposite responses that correspond to excitation and inhibition. Some of them are persistent intrusions of stressful ideas into consciousness—excitatory processes. Others are denials—inhibition— of the same ideas. Table 5.1 presents this opposition in a way that reveals once more the usefulness of the cognition-affect-reaction tendency analysis of the elements of behavior.

Summary and Conclusions

Most behavior reflects a blend of opposing excitatory and inhibitory influences. The stimuli that evoke the neural processes that translate into the experience of a certain color also activate the processes for the complement of that color. Noxious stimulation elicits, but also numbs, the experience of pain. In conditioning, stimuli and responses that lead to reinforcement result in excitation; omitting reinforcement leads to inhibition, a fact that has important implications for the controls required to demonstrate the existence of conditioning (Rescorla 1967).

The outcomes of studies of negative afterimages in vision, the time course of emotion, and several phenomena of classical conditioning support four general hypotheses about the action of and interaction between excitation and inhibition:

1. Inhibition and excitation are inseparably linked. The existence of one process means that the other is also there.
2. The relation between excitation and inhibition is subtractive. The net influence of the two processes on behavior depends on the difference in their magnitudes. When inhibition is greater than excitation, the strength of instigation can be negative.
3. Excitation acts more rapidly than inhibition. Stimuli attract attention before inhibition (not quite totally) excludes most of those that bombard the individual. In a very much more complicated

Table 5.1
Opposed Reactions to Stress

	Excitation	Inhibition
Cognition	Confusion	Dimming of attention
	Feelings of unreality	Dazed and cloudy consciousness
	Preoccupation with stressful events	Avoidance of attending
	Sudden thoughts that interfere with ongoing activities	Inability to concentrate or to see the significance of events or obvious logical connections
	Inability to stop such rumination once it starts	Memory failure
	Intellectualization of emotional problems	Blocking of stressful thoughts through fantasy
	Vivid "flashbulb memories" of traumatic experiences	Avoidance of associations to stressful ideas
		Denial
		Claiming that obvious meanings are not true
		Repression of the traumatic experiences
Affect	Unbidden intense sensations irrelevant to the situation	
	Hyperexcitability	
	Tension and alertness—the feeling of being "keyed up"	
	Excessive appetite	
	Pangs of emotion that well up and subside with little connection to the real world	
	Excitation	Inhibition
	Irritability	Emotional numbness: lowered emotional reactivity
	Aggression	Sense of not having feelings or appropriate emotions
	Hostility	
	Loss of "joy of living"	Loss of appetite
	Nightmares	Flattened affect (lack of emotion)
	Fear and free-floating anxiety	
	Guilt at having survived while others perished	
	Depression	
Reaction tendency	Hypervigilance: excessive alertness, tense expectancy, trembling, nervous tics, bruxism (grinding the teeth)	Retarded motor action
		Apathetic nonresponsiveness
	Hypermobility: restless moving about, impulsive behavior, an overpowering urge to run or cry	Fatigue
	Enhanced startle reactions	
	Flinching or blanching to stimuli that do not warrant such reactions	
	Insomnia	
	Accident proneness	

Sources: Horowitz 1986; Selye 1976.

context, our rejection of false statements begins with automatic acceptance of their truth, until further processing leads us to deny them (Gilbert, Krull, and Malone 1990).

4. Excitation and inhibition both persist in time, following the events that create them. When a colored stimulus disappears, a brief, positive afterimage remains, and the negative afterimage that follows lasts even longer. Similar sequences of events occur in emotion and classical conditioning.

Proviso: Both the absolute and relative strengths of excitation and inhibition depend on the context of their occurrence. The most important component of this proviso is that cognitive involvement may have a powerful inhibitory influence on behavior. In infants, attention inhibits reflex action, and in adult college students, even minor cognitive involvement inhibits performance in classical conditioning experiments.

The excitation-inhibition interaction has survival value because it tends to promote behavior that is adaptive and to exclude behavior that is maladaptive. In terms of the ideas developed in chapter 4, the alertness-numbing sequence of reactions to noxious stimulation favors *coping* as a first response to diminish suffering, a form of *adaptation*, when coping is impossible. It is much to our benefit that attention sifts information through a "smart filter" as material passes from sensation to awareness

As Pavlov noted in his discussions of temperament, nonhuman animals exhibit individual differences in the balance of excitation and inhibition. At the human level, such differences appear as variations in such attributes as extroversion (introversion) and sensitization (repression). Where people fall on these dimensions determines how they deal with stress.

The classification of the schizophrenias that distinguishes negative-symptom schizophrenia from positive-symptom schizophrenia (Andreasen 1985) might be called "inhibitory" and "excitatory" schizophrenia. Negative symptoms are deficits, such as flattened affect, apathy, and social withdrawal. Positive symptoms are those that add something to behavior and experience, such as emotional turmoil, delusions, hallucinations, motor excitement, and disturbances of speech.

Chapter 6
Thresholds for Responding

The materials covered in the two previous chapters of this book begin to come together in this one. As Peter Killeen describes such a synthesis, "Human behavior is a complex blend of habitual responses and creative acts [adaptations and copings]. Attempts to deal with [excite] either of these two components of behavior often proceed by denying [inhibiting] the reality of one or minimizing the importance of the other [and] negative feedback [inhibition produced by excitation] keeps the system in check until perturbations exceed a threshold" (Killeen 1989, p. 53). In this chapter I review the history of the threshold concept, present some of its applications, and then explain how the system described in chapter 3 turns potentials into behavior.

Historical Introduction

The British empiricists' emphasis on the sensory origins of knowledge led them to ask two questions: What, for any sensory modality, is the weakest stimulus an individual can detect? And, for any attribute of these sensations, what is the smallest detectable difference in stimulation? These questions ask, respectively, about the absolute and difference thresholds of sensory experience.

Absolute Threshold
In one method of determining the absolute threshold, over a series of trials the experimenter presents a sequence of stimuli that increase in intensity on some trials and decrease on others, and the observer reports whether he or she detects each stimulus. The probability of a positive response in these experiments increases as is shown in figure 6.1. By convention, the absolute threshold is the intensity of stimulation that an observer detects on half the trials.

Difference Threshold
Difference thresholds had a very special meaning for the structural psychologists, who were the direct descendants of the empiricist philosophers. The structuralists believed that the smallest detectable dif-

ferences in sensory experience are mental atoms—the particles of consciousness. The purpose of psychophysical research was to determine the values of these difference thresholds, or just noticeable differences (JNDs), for all of the sensory dimensions of experience: quality (color, pitch), intensity, duration, and extent (area) of stimulation.

In a typical experiment to determine the difference threshold, the experimenter presents an observer with two stimuli: a standard stimulus, followed by a test stimulus with a different value of the attribute of interest. The magnitude of the difference between the two stimuli varies from trial to trial, and on each trial, the observer reports whether he or she detects that difference. The results are like those shown in figure 6.1, except that the baseline becomes a measure of the difference between a standard stimulus and a test stimulus. The smallest separation stimulus that the observer detects half of the time is the difference threshold—the JND.

Weber's Law   In the 1830s, Ernst Heinrich Weber (1795–1878) proposed that JNDs are relative: the stronger the standard stimulus is, the greater is the difference threshold, and he described this relationship in a mathematical formula, called Weber's law:

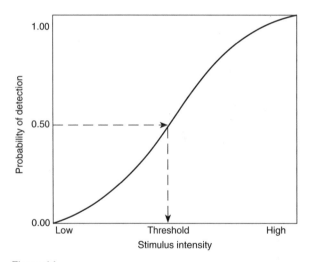

Figure 6.1
The Definition of the Absolute Threshold
The probability of detecting a stimulus (vertical axis) is plotted against stimulus intensity (horizontal axis). The absolute threshold is the intensity of stimulation that has a .5 probability of detection. The two arrows show the calculations. With the horizontal axis representing differences in stimulation, a similar figure describes the data obtained in experiments designed to determine difference thresholds.

$\Delta I / I = K,$

where ΔI is the difference threshold or JND, I is the intensity of the standard stimulus, and K ("Weber's fraction") is a constant that depends on the particular psychological and physical dimensions being investigated. Tests of Weber's law, which determined the sizes of JNDs at several levels of stimulation, revealed that the Weber fraction is constant over a wide range of stimuli, but when stimuli are extremely weak or very strong, actual JNDs are larger than Weber's law predicts.

Fechner's Law   Some years later, Gustav Fechner (1801–1878) enlarged on Weber's contribution and proposed what came to be known as Fechner's law, relating the intensity of sensory experience to the intensity of stimulation. Fechner's law depended on the assumptions that (1) Weber's law is true, (2) JNDs are the basic units of sensation, (3) at every level of physical stimulation JNDs represent equal increments of sensory experience, (4) the absolute threshold is the zero point on a scale of sensory intensity, (5) JNDs are additive, and (6) the intensity of any sensory experience is the total of all the JNDs between the absolute threshold and the stimulus responsible for the experience whose intensity is being measured.

Mathematically, the first of these assumptions means that the function relating increases in the intensity of experience to the intensity of stimulation must be logarithmic. It cannot be linear because as the intensity of stimulation increases, greater and greater increases in stimulation are required to produce a JND. The usual statement of Fechner's law is:

$S = K \log I + A,$

where S is the intensity of sensory experience, I is stimulus intensity, A is the absolute threshold, and K is a constant related to the Weber fraction.

Functions of Thresholds in Psychology

Fechner's logarithmic law illustrates one of several roles that thresholds play in psychology. They provide measures that recognize the nonlinear relationship between the values of dependent and independent variables that is typical of biological and psychological functions. Hovland's (1937) representation of sound frequencies in terms of JNDs on the baseline of graphs of stimulus generalization is an application of this idea. Informally, psychologists employ the same strategy whenever they express time or stimulus intensity in terms of log units, a practice that is common in research on learning, memory, and reaction time.

Threshold as Defining Operations
Another useful purpose that thresholds serve in psychology is the definition of important concepts. Without being identified as such, the concept of absolute threshold defines such other concepts as statistical significance, where the absolute threshold is an accepted probability that a statistic is not an accident of sampling; critical mass, the threshold number of participants required for programs to be effective; and clinical depression, where a patient's symptoms have to meet set of standard criteria to justify that diagnosis.

In a more formal application, figure 6.2 presents three functions of the type obtained for the items on age scales of intelligence. Each curve is for a single item, with the chronological ages of groups of children represented on the baseline and the percentage of the children in those groups who passed that item on the vertical axis. The curves have the same form as figure 6. 1. The downward arrows show that the method

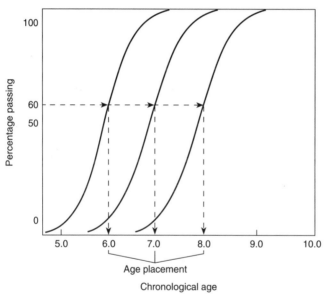

Figure 6.2
Placement of Items on an Age Scale of Intelligence as an Application of the Threshold Concept
These are hypothetical data of the type obtained when a large group of children who vary in chronological age (horizontal axis) from 5.0 to 10.0 years are tested with items that are being considered for inclusion in a test like the Stanford-Binet test of intelligence. The percentage of children who pass the item (vertical axis) increases with age. Items are acceptable only if the function is steep enough to indicate discrimination among children of different ages. Acceptable items appear on the test at an age level where about 60 percent of the test children pass them.

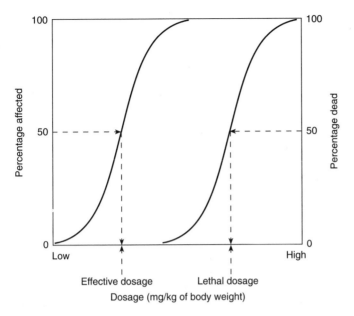

Figure 6.3
Effective and Lethal Dose Curves as Threshold Functions
Animals receiving increasingly large dosages (e.g., milligrams of drug per kilogram of body weight, horizontal axis) show increasing probabilities of being affected in some particular way (e.g., loss of motor control, left-hand vertical axis) or dying (right-hand axis). The effective and lethal thresholds may be defined in terms of any percentage of these consequences that seems appropriate. The graph employs a 50 percent criterion. Note that some animals are unaffected by dosages that are lethal for others.

for determining the mental age placement of these items was the same as the method used to define an absolute threshold of sensation. From the point on each function where about 60 percent of the children passed the item, an arrow to the baseline defined the placement of that item.

The two functions in figure 6.3 are effective and lethal dose curves for a drug. They show the percentage of animals affected by and killed by increasing dosages of that drug. The downward arrows from the 50 percent points on these curves provide definitions of effective and lethal dosages of the drug. You will note that dosages that leave some animals unaffected are fatal to some others.

These last observations make a point that is as important as the facts that they communicate. Absolute thresholds are less absolute than that term implies. Nothing in the data prevents a definition of the absolute and difference thresholds (figure 6.1) in terms of a 25 percent or 75 percent rate of detection instead of 50 percent. Indeed, in figure 6.2 the downward arrows are from 60 percent passing, rather than 50 percent as might be expected on the assumption that the mental age placement of an item should be the chronological age of the average child who passes it. This adjustment is an informal correction for the unrepresentativeness of the samples used to standardize these tests. There were too few children at the lower end of the continuum of intelligence.

"Thresholds" in Correlational Psychology
Although psychophysics is most intimately a part of experimental psychology, the concepts of that field have important messages for the psychology of tests and measures. In particular, they can bring badly needed clarity to controversies that surround the practical uses of such tests as the ACT and SAT to admit applicants to college. A picture of the situation of tests and other measures in psychology's second science appears in figure 6.4.

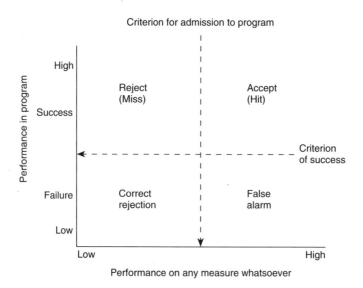

Figure 6.4
Realities of Selecting Individuals for Programs
Think of this figure as a correlational scatter plot. Scores on a test or some other measure are arranged from low to high on the horizontal axis. Measures of performance in the program for which selection is being made are ordered, from low to high, on the vertical axis. The criteria are set at the points on both dimensions that do as good a job as possible, given the number of applicants available, of maximizing the number of "hits" and minimizing the number of "false positives" among the applicants accepted, but no matter where the criteria are set, the four subgroups of applicants remain—unless the validity of the test is perfect.

Any measure whatsoever that sets a standard for selecting people for a program defines a threshold. It divides applicants into two groups: those who are accepted because they meet the standard (exceed the threshold) and those who are rejected because they do not. Performance in the program, then, divides each of these two groups into two subgroups: for the accepted individuals, those who are successful and unsuccessful in the program; for the individuals rejected, those who would have failed or succeeded had they been accepted. In both cases, the line dividing success from failure is a threshold.

In the language of signal detectability, the two subgroups of accepted applicants who, respectively, succeed and fail are "hits" and "false alarms." Of the applicants rejected, those who would have been successful if they had been admitted are the "misses." Those who would have failed are "correct rejections." These last two groups exist only out of logical necessity. Because they were rejected, their success or failure cannot be observed directly.

Now these points: (1) Figure 6.4 presents an inescapable reality; it exists for any measure one can think of. In the case of selecting applicants to college, switching from the SAT and ACT to letters of recommendation, as is sometimes recommended, would not change the situation in any important way; it is just that the criterion for selection (threshold) would be on a different measure. (2) However carried out, selection always is unfair to someone. It robs the rejected "misses" of an experience of success; the accepted "false alarms" suffer from their failure in a program that is inappropriate for them, and they impede the progress of the candidates who belong there. (3) The only way to reduce the damage is to improve the validity of the measures, something that usually has not been done for the recommended alternatives to standardized tests.

The Threshold of Consciousness

In what may have been the first American experiment in psychology, C. S. Peirce (1839–1914) and Joseph Jastrow (1863–1944), serving as their own subjects, obtained data for the existence of a phenomenon that would come to be called "subception," "subliminal perception," "unconscious perception," and "implicit perception." They forced themselves to decide which of two pressures or visual intensities that differed by less than a JND was heavier or brighter and to rate the confidence of their judgments on a four-point scale. Although the differences between the stimuli and the standard were all subthreshold, they represented three degrees of this subliminal difference. Because the differences were so small, Peirce and Jastrow had no confidence in their judgments. Surprisingly, however, their reports were correct about 65 percent of the time, and their accuracy varied directly with the magnitude of the actual difference in stimulation (Peirce and Jastrow 1884).

This demonstration should have been convincing, but the concept of unconscious influences on behavior needed another century to establish credibility. The classical behaviorists objected to such conceptions because unconscious influences were not observable and seemed beyond the pale of natural science. Even William James, who usually was receptive to such thinking, was negative. In *Principles of Psychology*, he toyed with the notion of exploiting the threshold concept in the interest of defining a subthreshold, unconscious mind, and he cited modern-sounding arguments for that idea: Automatic habits must reside somewhere, so why not in the unconscious? Mental activity exists outside awareness: "We know more than we can say. Our conclusions run ahead of our power to analyze their grounds" (James 1890a, 1:167). And "we deliberately analyze our motives, and find that at bottom they contain jealousies and cupidities that we little suspected to be there" (1:170). In spite of those persuasions, James rejected the concept of unconscious mental life because "it is the sovereign means for believing what one likes in psychology, and turning what might become a science into a tumbling-ground for whimsies" (1:163).

Since then, the world has changed. The scientific status of the assumption of unconscious influences on behavior is now generally accepted, but with the recognition that concepts that convey that notion—subliminal perception, unconscious motivation, repressed anxiety—are intervening variables. Like any other of these concepts, they are acceptable if their defining operations and effects on behavior can be specified. The chief thing that distinguishes unconscious influences from conscious ones is the nature of these behavioral effects. The usual evidence that shows that a stimulus is above threshold is a subject's self-report. Demonstrations of unconscious influences on behavior typically involve stimuli and responses that they cannot report.

Psychology has now demonstrated the existence of subliminal effects in diverse contexts. The distinctions between implicit and explicit memory and a parallel distinction in perception are well established. The heuristics (also known as mental sets) that sometimes aid and sometimes frustrate problems solving are usually unconscious. Unconscious motivation is a scientific fact, if only because people are unaware of the set points and other physiological mechanisms that control the basic drives. The behavioral method of systematic desensitization achieves its therapeutic results by crowding, but not crossing, the threshold of anxiety.

Beyond the Upper Limits of Instigation

Some experiments in psychophysics have demonstrated that in addition to their lower thresholds, sensations have an upper limit. Above a certain level, higher intensities of sound, light, and pressure produce pain instead of hearing, touch, or vision. The concept reappears in many psychobiological contexts. Pavlov believed that classical conditioning increases with CS intensity up to the "top capability" of the cortical cells, where a process of negative induction takes over, and stimuli of still greater intensity are less and less effective. In cognitive psychology, the concept of processing capacity is an upper threshold, beyond which added inputs produce information overload. In the workplace, job requirements put an upper limit on the talent that produces optimal performance. An employee who has more intelligence than a job requires may be careless and distractible and less effective than someone not so bright. More generally, it appears that increments in the magnitudes of many independent variables beyond a certain limit do more than merely augment a single reaction; they lead to qualitative changes in the kind of influence that increases in these conditions have on behavior.

The Yerkes-Dodson Law   On many tasks the relationship between performance and arousal is nonmonotonic. As the level of activation increases, performance increases and then decreases. This inverted-U relationship is commonly known as the Yerkes-Dodson law, after an early demonstration by Yerkes and Dodson (1908) that the speed of discrimination learning increases and then decreases with increasing levels of motivation. The usual interpretation of such data is that for any task, there is an optimal level of arousal and that less-than-optimal levels reduce performance—nothing more than that.

Revised Interpretation   One problem with that type of analysis is that it makes no adaptive sense for high levels of arousal to lead the organism to adapt less effectively. A more reasonable explanation is that as motivation increases, the strength of a dominant response increases, and beyond some optimal point, it becomes so strong that it robs the individual of the flexibility required to perform effectively.

The ancient *Umweg* (detour) experiment shows the mechanism clearly. In these experiments, an animal, often a chicken, sees through a wire fence food that it can obtain by going around the end of the fence. This is an easy problem unless the chicken is very hungry. In that case, it tries so hard to go to the food directly through the fence that the problem becomes difficult.

In addition to producing such inflexibilities, heightened arousal leads to behavior that is irrelevant to the task at hand. Consider the psychological situation of college students, who are usually good at taking tests. Faced with a difficult examination, they feel mounting nervousness because a bad grade may mean failure. Their anxiety finds expression in a set of useless and destructive thoughts: "What if I fail?" "What will my professor think of this rotten performance?" "How can I ever tell my parents?" "Are my chances of admission to medical school down the toilet?" "Why am I such a worthless person?" When such reactions happen, performance on the test—which would have benefited from a more modest increase in motivation—will deteriorate.

Thresholds as Response Criteria

Contrary to a common way of speaking, thresholds are not a property of stimuli. They are properties of organisms, criteria that determine whether a particular stimulus elicits a response. A resting neuron fires when the intensity of stimulation exceeds a value that is a property of the neuron. A subject responds yes in any trial in a psychophysical experiment when experience exceeds his or her criterion for responding positively in such situations. Stress brings on a stress reaction when environmental irritations reach a person's breaking point. Many other examples fit this pattern, which implies that instigation must reach a threshold to elicit a reaction: the certainty required for a witness to report a certain memory about a crime; the standards people use for self-disclosure; the criteria employed to make the quasi-quantitative judgments that things are old, many, far away, or large, and the qualitative judgments that things are beautiful, just, good, or boring; the amount of credibility required to make communication believable; and, for insulting comments, the intensity of insult needed to conclude that "them's fightin' words."

Returning now to one of the examples just mentioned, figure 6.5, depicting the diasthesis-stress model of psychopathology, puts this idea into a graphic form that has widespread applicability. The baseline of figure 6.6 represents the predispositions (potential) of different individuals for the development of a behavioral disorder; the vertical axis is a measure of the strengths of the stressors (instigations) in their lives. The curve is a threshold function. It divides the graphic space into two regions, which correspond to healthy and unhealthy stress reactions. This model implies that everyone has a breaking point: all of us will fail to function adequately when stress is strong enough. Figure 6.6 demonstrates that this threshold model can describe the interactions that bring expression to a variety of potentials.

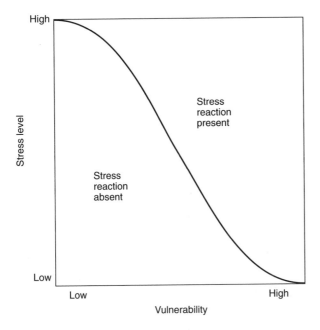

Figure 6.5
The Diasthesis-Stress Model
We all spend our days somewhere in the space defined by this graph. The baseline is
our predisposition, or vulnerability, to psychopathology. It remains fairly stable over
time. The vertical axis is the amount of stress we are under at any moment. Sometimes
it is low, sometimes high. The curved line is a stress threshold. Reading from the baseline, up from the value corresponding to a person's vulnerability, any stress below the
threshold is one with which the individual can cope. Any stress above the threshold is
one that produces a stress reaction. The threshold is like the plimsoll mark on a ship—
the horizontal line that indicates the load the ship can safely carry. Loads that force the
ship deeper into the water are dangerous.

The Elicitation of Behavior

The ideas developed in the previous pages are the raw materials I need
to keep the promise in the first paragraph of this chapter: to show
how the concepts of excitation, inhibition, and threshold operate in the
elicitation of behavior. In order to fulfill that obligation, I must develop
the background for an argument that is a departure from traditional
perspectives.

The Heritage of Newton

Throughout its history, Newtonian mechanics has been psychology's
role model. The various systems, theories, and schools that have punctuated the history of psychology fit that pattern. They differed in their

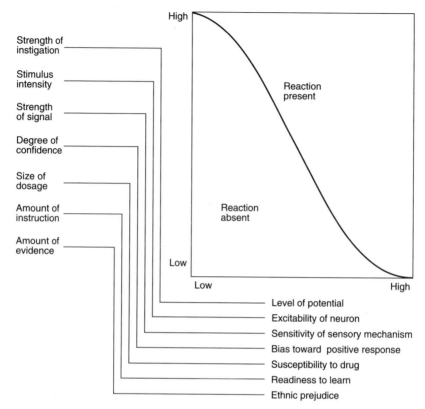

Figure 6.6

The Threshold Model in Several Contexts

This figure shows that, in general, the greater the potential is for a given type of reaction (horizontal axis), the less is the instigation required (vertical axis) to evoke a response. The terms that head the lists on the two axes of the graph, *level of potential* and *strength of instigation,* are general categories. The other items in the list are examples. The function within these axes, labeled *threshold,* divides the bounded space into two regions. Read the figure as you would a correlational scatter plot. Combinations of potential and instigation above the threshold initiate a reaction; those below the threshold do not. From top to bottom, the specific reactions represented are neural action potentials, absolute sensory thresholds, "yes" responses in any situation where the theory of signal detectability applies, effective and lethal dosages of drugs, "critical periods" in learning, and racial and other ethnic prejudice.

surface features, but the underlying structures all had the form of Newton's hypothetico-deductive model.

Newton's physics has had great success in dealing with the behavior of falling objects, balls rolling down inclined planes, the tides, and the planets in their orbits. Given quantitative values of the variables controlling these events, that science predicts them almost exactly. There are other happenings, however, that Newtonian physics cannot predict: anything to do with turbulence, the weather, water coming from a spigot, the detailed composition of a heartbeat, the brainstorm of an epileptic seizure—even the "spontaneous" firing of a single neuron.

The new sciences of catastrophe and chaos theory (Gleick 1987) deal with such events. One point of emphasis in these theories is that, for some phenomena, tiny differences in initial states multiply; they create a chain reaction, and the "same" starting conditions have different outcomes. The official metaphor is "the butterfly effect": a butterfly flaps its wings in Tokyo, and the weather in London is different. Such differences may appear abruptly, as though they resulted from the crossing of a threshold.

These discontinuities occur in many real-world situations. Water on the stove begins to bubble when its slowly rising temperature reaches the local boiling point; alternatively, as the temperature lowers, water suddenly is crystalline. The continued torturing of the materials that certain airplanes are made of slowly weakens them, so that stresses they once withstood now tear their engines off, with untold costs in human lives.

Such huge effects of small, antecedent influences are hard to reconcile with Newton's second law of motion, which postulates a proportional relationship between the magnitudes of the causes of physical events and their consequences: "The change of motion is proportional to the motive force impressed; and is made in the direction of the right line in which the force is impressed" (Cajori 1947, p. 13). There is a similar difficulty for psychology, which, implicitly adopting this Newtonian axiom, tends to expect the changes in behavior that occur with practice, increasing age, and mounting environmental stress to be gradual. Thus, insightful learning, developmental stages, and psychopathologies with sudden onsets—the existence of all these phenomena was established long ago—create problems for the traditional science of psychology. Perhaps the assumption drawn from modern physics—that accumulating little causes can bring potentials for behavior to a strength that carries them across a threshold—is the key to understanding such phenomena.

The Additivity of Subthreshold Influences
William James proposed that small influences accumulate in his discussion of the "tensions" in neural activity "which at last overcome a resistance" (James 1890a, 1:82). And, characteristically, he went on to offer several applications to psychology: "If we are striving to remember a lost name or fact, we think of as many 'cues' as possible, so that by their joint action they may recall what no one of them can recall alone," and, "A strange person and darkness, are both of them stimuli to fear and mistrust in dogs. . . . Neither circumstance alone may awaken outward manifestation, but together, i.e. when the strange man is met in the dark, the dog will be excited to violent defiance" (1:84–85).

Examples from Traditional Psychology   The literature in psychology provides a multitude of examples of behavior that comes about as a result of the gradual accumulation of smaller influences. Although the energies that stimulate the senses come in graded quantities, many perceptual events are all or none. When the acoustic stimulus for "ba" changes gradually to that for "da"—in steps that the nervous system is capable of registering but consciousness is not—auditory perception does not shift until it changes all at once. In avoidance learning based on traumatic punishment (Solomon and Wynne 1954), dogs frequently make their first successful avoidance responses suddenly, after many trials on which they could do no better than escape, although they were surely learning. In Japanese school violence (*Ijime*), a group of tormentors pick on a single victim—nothing violent, just a relentless series of little insults and other torments, but the effects accumulate, sometimes with tragic consequences. In one highly publicized case, an adolescent boy committed suicide, leaving a note, naming the tormentors and saying that they knew why he had killed himself (Reiko Mazuka, personal communication, 1994).

Examples from Neuropathology   In the 1960s, neurosurgeons working with chronic animal preparations developed a technique for "kindling" epileptic seizures, by delivering to the brain a series of weak electric shocks. At first, the shocks had no effect, but a series of them evoked a limited seizure. With continued stimulation at the same site, the animals exhibited a widespread seizure consisting of chewing, nodding their heads, and extending their paws in a spasm. With time these seizures came on spontaneously; the intervals between them diminished, and the symptoms become more severe.

This pattern parallels the usual history of what are now called bipolar affective disorders. Emil Kraeplin (1856–1926), the giant in the history of descriptive psychiatry, noted in the nineteenth century that this disorder typically begins early in life with a single episode, usually of depression. After that, there is a progression of increasingly severe episodes, with decreasing intervals between them, and a diminishing requirement for external trauma to produce the symptoms. Eventually patients with this disorder switch back and forth from ecstatic euphoria to deep depression rapidly, either spontaneously or in response to trivial provocations.

The General Adaptation Syndrome   Selye's pioneering work with laboratory rats on the general adaptation syndrome (GAS) demonstrated that reactions to continuing stress occur in stages of alarm, resistance, and exhaustion. This sequence occurs because the effects of stress are additive. As stress continues, it takes the animal upward on the Y axis of figure 6.5—which, to represent the GAS, needs separate functions for alarm, resistance, and exhaustion—and above the threshold level of instigation for each of these potential reactions.

Selye also obtained more direct evidence for the additive property of stress. A new stressor delivered in the stage of resistance, when the animals were effectively adapting—in my terminology, "coping" would be the wrong word—brought them prematurely to the stage of exhaustion, and many of them died earlier than they would have without the added stress.

These phenomena appear to have some generality. Human reactions to disasters like floods, tornadoes, and the Hiroshima bombing also proceed in stages—often three of them that bear a qualitative resemblance to the general adaptation syndrome. Further evidence at the human level that the effects of stress are cumulative comes from the frequency with which war veterans react to personal difficulties with a posttraumatic stress disorder.

Temporary Stabilities in Behavior
Progress through the sequence of stress reactions is far from orderly, however. Some people never break down, and others maintain a precarious adjustment for extended periods, until a new stressor pushes them over their threshold for a stress reaction. The origin of this uncertainty is that stress evokes protective mechanisms, just as painful stimulation brings insensitivity to pain. These forces grow together and balance one another. The result is a fragile equilibrium, which may give way to another. Peter Killeen (1989) quotes James Clerk Maxwell, who saw great generality in such temporary balances: "The rock loosened by frost and balanced on a singular point of the mountain-side, the little spark which kindles the great forest, the little word which sets the world fighting, the little scruple which prevents a man from

doing his will, the little spore which blights all the potatoes, the little gemmule which makes us philosophers or idiots. Every instance above a certain rank [reaches a threshold]. At these points, influences whose physical magnitude is too small to be taken account of by a finite being, may produce results of the greatest importance."

To Maxwell's examples, one might add the subliminal genotypic changes that produce the stagelike pattern of organic evolution called punctuated equilibrium; the physical stability of species living in a stable environment and the rapid evolution that occurs with environmental change; the homeostatic balances of many physiological reactions; the heightened effective and lethal thresholds for drugs that occur with long abuse; and, particularly apt for psychology, the wavering indecision of an individual in an approach-avoidance conflict at the point where the tendency to approach an ambivalent goal object is exactly balanced by the tendency to avoid it.

From Potential to Performance

The principle of response elicitation suggested by the content of this chapter is that behavior happens when a potential exceeds a threshold. In theory, this suprathreshold strength of potentials might come about because of an increase in the strength of a potential, a decrease in a threshold for reaction, or both.

Recall that instigation initiates opposed companion processes: rapid-acting excitation and slower-acting inhibition. My tentative hypothesis is that, in the main, excitation increases potentials and inhibition lowers thresholds. These effects are detectable in their influences on different measures of "the same" behavior: lowered thresholds increase the probability of a reaction; increased potentials increase the vigor, particularly the speed of the response. Ancient data on the low correlations between the frequency and latency of conditioned reflexes (about $-.25$) support the conclusion that these measures reflect different underlying mechanisms (Hilgard and Marquis 1940, p. 138). In the same vein, "While the testimony of the literature is not unequivocal, much of the evidence points to an influence of drive [excitation] on speed and rate of response measures but not on errors or correct responses" (Cofer and Appley 1964, p. 521).

In a series of brilliant studies, Lynn Hasher, Rose Zacks, and their colleagues (Hasher 1994; Zacks and Hasher 1994) have obtained data that show how the inhibitory influences operate in working (short-term) memory. A part of their interpretation translates easily into an effect on thresholds. They see inhibition behaving like Freud's "censor," and shutting out of consciousness inputs that do not contribute to such goals as comprehension. The effect of inhibition is exceedingly pervasive. Within working memory, inhibition suppresses the irrelevant information that succeeds in getting there, as well as information that becomes irrelevant when those goals change. It provides the "mental sets" that hold prepotent responses in a state of readiness while competing ones are judged for their appropriateness to current purposes.

One of the results of normal aging is a weakening of inhibition. By comparison with younger people, the working memories of the elderly contain more irrelevant information because, with inhibition weakened, such inputs have easier access to consciousness. As a result, older people are distractible and prone to error. They are less able to maintain a focus of attention, and their traffic accident rates are elevated. Within working memory, this same irrelevant information has an impact on ideation and behavior, because inhibiting mechanisms are not so easily engaged. Sometimes in conversation, older people impulsively express embarrassing ideas without monitoring them for propriety or inhibiting those that are inappropriate. Their memories suffer from the powerful and much-studied pro- and retroactive interfering effects of extraneous associations. The deficient inhibition of the elderly is less than totally disastrous, however. Their rich associations represent a breadth of knowledge that sometimes provide them with solutions—even creative solutions—to problems that younger people never think of.

Summary and Conclusions

The science of psychology began with psychophysics, as an exploration of the consequences of the empiricist assumption that the origins of human knowledge are in sensory experience ("psycho") produced by stimulation ("physics"). The important questions were about the absolute and difference thresholds of sensation. Many of the current methods of psychology and much of its thinking are descendants of research in that tradition. The concept of absolute threshold has applications that range from the activities of single neurons to the etiology of stress reactions. It is the central idea in definitions of lethal and effective dosages of drugs and in the appropriate level for items on age-scale measures of intelligence.

In all these applications, it is important to recognize that the concept of absolute threshold is an intervening variable that links an independent variable, stimulus intensity, to a measure of behavior, typically the detection of a signal on 50 percent of an individual's opportunities to do so. Such thinking has led to the rehabilitation of the concept of

unconscious influences on behavior. Present-day research on subliminal perception, implicit memory, and unconscious motivation owes its
legitimacy to this interpretation.

It is particularly worth noting that the threshold concept has found
its way into the psychology of tests and measures, where it fits the
model employed in theories of signal detectability, which translate that
concept into a criterion for responding. Applications of such theorizing
to the use of tests for selecting individuals for programs of training
and education provide the basis for clearer thinking in an area where
it often is desperately needed.

The first highlight in the history of the concept of the difference
threshold was Weber's discovery that JNDs in sensation are relative.
The second was Fechner's formulation of a law describing how JNDs
add to produce intensities of experience that vary with the logarithm
of stimulus intensity. This law marks the beginning of measurement
in psychology.

Fechner's assumption that JNDs are additive has a subtler presence
in psychology today. Supported by the recognition that almost any
kind of increasing instigation alters individuals' repertoires of responses, it aids our understanding of the many discontinuities in
behavior. Psychological development, complex learning, and the evolution of psychopathology all follow such a pattern. These reactions
reflect the gradual development of many separate potentials that are
unlikely to grow in synchrony. Sometimes those that mature first have
to wait for others to catch up, and once they do catch up, it takes time
for them to get their act together. While this is going on, there will be
little evidence of change. In maturation, there will be stages; the transi-
tion from one stage to the next may be abrupt. In learning there will
be plateaus; the shift to better performance may seem insightful. Psychopathological reactions may have an insidious onset; the appearance
of the illness in response to stress may look like a "nervous breakdown." These changes in behavior often are components of a long-
term pattern of intermittent stabilities, punctuated by periods of
rapid change.

The general principle suggested by the content of this chapter is that
behavior happens when a potential exceeds a threshold, an outcome
that occurs as a result of increases in the strengths of potentials and
decreases in thresholds. The main effects of increased potentials and
decreased thresholds are on different measures of behavior: lowered
thresholds increase response probabilities; increased potentials increase the vigor of responses.

An application of this distinction brings an important insight to our
understanding of human aging. By comparison with younger people,

the inhibitory processes are weaker in the elderly. As a result, older people are distractible, impulsive, and less able to maintain a focus of attention. Their memories suffer from the effects of extraneous associations. The bright spot in this picture is that their weakened inhibition sometimes lead older people to creative solutions for problems that younger people never think of.

Chapter 7

Organized and Disorganized Behavior

The phenomenon of organization appears to be a fundamental fact of nature. The tiniest disruption of the organization of a soap bubble destroys the whole completely. When one species of organism goes extinct, the whole ecosystem changes. In classical conditioning, a principle of "belongingness" determines the ease with which—and possibly whether—associations can be established. In the psychology of perception, the Gestalt psychologists' figure-ground relationships and principles of grouping are powerful determiners of perception. Musical patterns survive and melodies remain even if a shift in key changes every note. Clustering and clusterings of clusters can extend the span of rote memory to several dozen items. Advance organizers and schemata are powerful allies of recall. The delusions of schizophrenic patients create a coherent, albeit crazy, world for them.

Organizational Processes and Their Sources

The fact that mental life is organized reminds us of the important point that if there is organization, there must be something elementary to organize. It also raises questions: What are the fundamental units of behavior and experience? What does the science of psychology know about the organizing processes that bring these elements together? Although complete answers to these questions are not available, certain facts are clear. The sensory receptors respond only to inputs like the quality, intensity, and duration of stimulation, and the neurons that they activate respond exclusively with impulses that vary only in their frequency. At a very basic level these must be the units out of which the complexities of mental life are created. There must be mechanisms that construct apples, enemies, dinosaurs, and strategies out of these materials.

Organizing Processes

The processes that produce the simplest visual organizations reveal patterns that repeat themselves in many contexts. In the retina, stimulation triggers both excitation and inhibition. Excitation in the receptive field of one ganglion cell produces inhibition in neighboring cells. These interactions enable the perception of sharply defined edges, lines, and contours.

Microcircuits in the brain and spinal cord respond to neural patterns like those just described as though they were elementary. According to the research of Hubel and Wiesel (1959), the receptive fields of certain cells in the visual cortex are specialized to react to such stimuli as lines of a particular width and length. Others respond to lines that are slanted at a certain angle or moving in a particular direction and at a certain speed.

Still other cells respond to entities that are more complex than lines and angles. There are cells in the brain of the macaque monkey that recognize the outline of a monkey's hand and a neural network in the human brain that has the ability to recognize people by their faces. Damage to certain areas of the brain leaves patients with prosopagnosia: although their perceptions of other objects are intact, they are unable to recognize human faces. As further evidence that this perception is the perception of something unitary, damage elsewhere in the brain may disrupt the visual perception of every object other than a face, but facial recognition remains unimpaired (Behrman, Moscovitch, and Winocur 1994).

Origins of Organization

These simplest (yet complicated) organizations are achieved by neural mechanisms that are almost certainly innate, a part of the "hard-wired" physiological endowment of organisms. Others come from experience. tHE fAcT ThAt, WitH lITtlE DiFfiCUlTy, Y0u CaN rEAd ThEse w0RdS, iN wHIcH tHe eLemENtS (tHe lETteRS) dIFfeR, points to the existence of one such organization that was acquired in the long and tedious process of learning how to read. The stimuli that make up the odd-looking phrase above excite the edge detectors in the retina and the specialized receptor cells in the visual cortex. The excitation of those cells initiates a part-to-whole mechanism—sometimes called data-driven or bottom-up processing—that suggests alternative hypotheses: the display might be words, numbers, random scribbles, or something else. Almost immediately, the observer unconsciously accepts one of these hypotheses, for example, that the display is a string of words and excludes (inhibits) all the others. Once adopted, expectations based on that hypothesis take over, and a whole-to-part—conceptually-driven or top-down—form of processing controls perception from that momemt on. Usually the result of top-down processing is accurate perception, but sometimes it produces misperceptions, for example, mistakes in reading proof, like the one that you just made if you happened to miss the spelling error in the previous sentence.

Hierarchical Organization The previous example also suggests a further point. The sentence contains different organizations that bear a hierarchical relationship to one another. The organization of lines into letters is subordinate to an organization of letters into words, which is subordinate to the organization of words into phrases, and phrases are subordinate to the structure of a sentence. Anders Ericsson, William Chase, and Steve Faloon (1980) traced the acquisition of such an organization in an experiment in which the subject, Steve Faloon, achieved a remarkable increase in his memory span for digits.

In this study Faloon tried to reproduce random numbers that were presented at the rate of one per second. If he got a sequence right, the next list was one digit longer; if he made a mistake, the next list was one digit shorter. The experiment went on for more than two years, providing Faloon with some 230 hours of practice. During the experiment, his memory span increased from seven digits (about average for college students) to more than eighty.

The details of Steve Faloon's performance show the development of a hierarchical three-level organization: chunks, groups of chunks, and supergroups (groups of groups of chunks). In the simplest organization, Faloon recoded the sequences of items into three- or four-digit chunks. He handled all but five or six digits in this way, storing those remaining items in a rehearsal buffer. For example, he remembered eighteen digits by recoding twelve of them into three chunks of four items each and holding the remaining six in the buffer. As the lists became longer and longer, Faloon began to develop a higher-level organization consisting of groups of chunks. One of them might be two four-digit chunks followed by two three-digit chunks. Finally he graduated to an even more complex organization involving groups of groups of chunks, which might consist of one group of three four-digit chunks, followed by another group of four three-digit chunks.

A graph of Faloon's performance over the hundreds of hours he practiced contains a series of plateaus, during which there was little or no improvement in his memory. These were periods when he was moving from one level of organization to a higher one, consolidating his gains and developing a new organization that led to increases in his digit span.

Although Faloon's performance is impressive, it seems less remarkable when you realize that you do something similar yourself. Think of the organization of the digits Faloon achieved as an eighty-letter, twenty-four-word numerical sentence, made up of telephone numbers (figure 7.1). The twenty-four words (chunks) are eight three-digit area codes (919), eight three-digit exchange numbers (684), and eight four-digit personal numbers (3904). The groups of chunks are complete numbers (919–684–3904), my office telephone number until it was

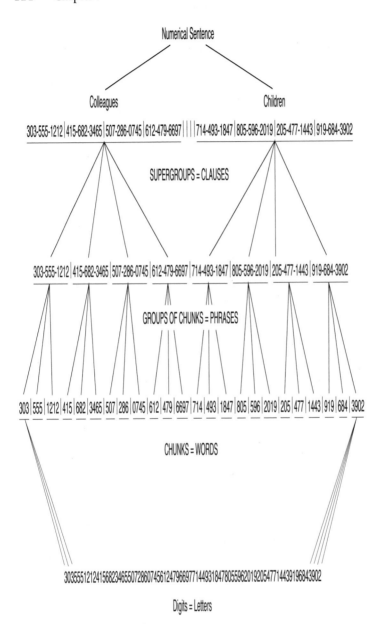

Figure 7.1
Three-Level Organization of Memory
This structure is similar to the one that Steve Faloon created to organize eighty digits. The chief difference is that the "rehearsal buffer" is not represented. To make the organization easy to perceive, the first group of chunks, corresponding to verbal phrases, is the telephone number for directory assistance in Colorado and the last is my former telephone number, mentioned in the discussion in the text.

changed a few years ago. The supergroups are phone numbers that belong together, such as those of your colleagues or your children who are attending different colleges.

The Role of Context   The hierarchical organization just described was one key to Faloon's expanded memory. His description of the mnemonic tactics he employed reveals a second that is different but related. Faloon was a good long-distance runner who had competed in races throughout the eastern United States, and he had amassed a store of trivia on running times and records for various races. He gave meaning to digit sequences by translating them into these terms. For example, 3492 was 3 minutes and 49.2 seconds, a near world-record time for the mile. Such strategies put memory into a specific context, providing it with an overarching framework, which is at the very top of the hierarchy of organizing influences.

Organized Cognition

Structures consisting of a hierarchical arrangement of more and more comprehensive organizations of elements within a certain context are evident throughout the subject matter of psychology. In perception, two of the Gestalt psychologists' principles of organization, proximity and similarity, produce visual groupings (figure 7.2a, b). The third principle of organization, good continuation, has effects that are more like those of context (figure 7.2c). Certain elements of that figure suggest plans of action that perception takes to completion. Perceptions of the two identical crescent moons in figure 7.2d show the effect of context in a more straightforward way: they control the meaning of perceptual elements. The meaning of the word "cardinal" changes in a similar way when it appears in the word strings: *sparrow, robin, bluebird, cardinal* versus *priest, pope, bishop, cardinal.*

Mental Representations of Knowledge

The understandings people have of many aspects of the world are organized hierarchically, in a structure that includes a context. When you read and comprehend a paragraph of text, your understanding relies heavily on a situation model (Kintsch 1994), which relates your previous knowledge to the topic of the text. When you recall the items of a shopping list that has no objective orgainization, your recollection employs a set of categories that form a hierarchy in which a general category at the top embraces increasingly specific subcategories. For example, from top to bottom, for the broad class of things called "beverages," this is one of several possible structures: (1) Beverages are (2)

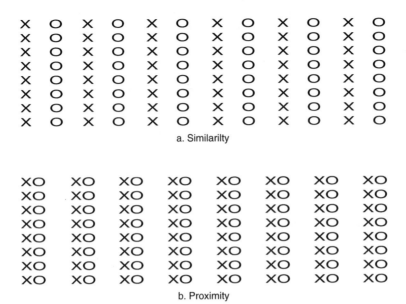

a. Similarilty

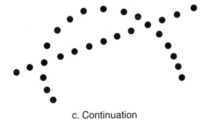

b. Proximity

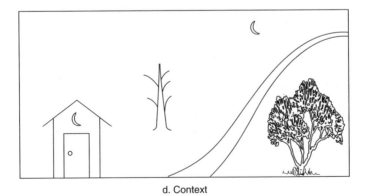

c. Continuation

d. Context

Figure 7.2
Gestalt Principles of Organization Create Chunks, and Context Controls Meaning

alcoholic or nonalcoholic; alcoholic beverages are (3) "hard" or "soft"; hard drinks include the (4) whiskies, gins, rums, and vodkas; whiskies may be (5) scotch, bourbon, rye, Irish, or Canadian; scotches are (6) single malts or blends; the single malts are (7) "smoky" or "non-smoky"; the "nonsmoky" scotches include (8) the Glenlivet, Glenfid-·dich, Glenmoranges, and Macallan; and so on.

Mnemonic Strategy
People use these organizations when they have things to remember. In currently popular terminology, hierarchical structures are the mental representations that people have of such knowledge, and recall is a process of model-based control. In an early demonstration of the role of organization in recall, Bousfield (1953) asked students to remember a list of sixty nouns that included exemplars of four categories: animals, vegetables, first names, and professions. Although the words were presented in a random order, the students tended to recall them by these categories, finishing one before they moved on to another.

Apparently memory occurs in the stages that are captured by the tip-of-the-tongue experience. First, people recall not the organization of knowledge but a single item that was included in that structure. That item prompts a recollection of the "representation" in terms of which information is stored—categories, a schema, or a theme. After that, other items come to mind, and people read out those they recognize as belonging to that structure, and they inhibit others.

Chase and Simon (1973) demonstrated similar strategies in a study that compared the memories of novices and expert chess players for pieces on a chessboard. These subjects inspected the positions of about twenty-five playing pieces on a board for five to ten seconds and then tried to reproduce their layout. On some trials, the configuration represented a meaningful situation in a game of chess; on others, the arrangement was at random. In either case, the novices could remember the locations of about six pieces, and the experts were no better when the placement of the pieces was random. When the arrangement was meaningful, however, the experts remembered about 90 percent of them. Their extensive playing experience helped them recognize the placement of several pieces (chunks) in terms of pattern they had encountered or made use of in actual games of chess, and they recalled them all together.

The Role of Context
Memories are tied to specific content and to situations. Chess masters are no better than anyone else in recalling nonchess information. With increasing age, people increasingly have problems remembering

names when they meet someone in an unfamiliar place. The phenomenon of encoding specificity is a laboratory demonstration of this failing. A subject trying to remember a list of words presented in the contexts provided by other words—for example, the word "black" presented after "train," with which it is weakly associated—may not even recognize "black" as a word in the to-be-remembered list when it is presented in a verbal context that represents a stronger associative connection: say, "white-black" (Tulving and Thompson 1973). There is even evidence that the contexts provided by a state of drunkenness (Weingartner et al. 1976) or a happy mood (Bower, Monteiro, and Gilligan 1978) are similarly beneficial to recall.

The Organization of Affect

In the psychology of motivation, Maslow's (1970) well-known theory is an organization of human needs into a hierarchical structure, in which those higher in the hierarchy become important only when lower needs are satisfied. The highest motive is a need for self-actualization; successively lower needs are those for self-esteem, love, safety, and physiological satisfaction.

As usual, William James anticipated this theory and used it to describe the functions of a hierarchically organized central nervous system: "The tramp who lives from hour to hour; the bohemian whose engagements are from day to day; the bachelor who builds but for a single life; the father who acts for another generation; the patriot who thinks of a whole community and many generations; and finally, the philosopher and saint whose cares are for humanity and for eternity,— these range themselves in an unbroken hierarchy, wherein each successive grade results from an increased manifestation of the special form of action by which the cerebral centres are distinguished from all below them" (James 1890a, 1:23)

The Structure of Personality
Combining elements of several definitions, personality is the organization of the traits that sets every individual apart from everybody else and determines how other people react to them. The traits are extremely numerous. English alone contains some 40,000 different trait-descriptive words that might conceivably refer to discrete elements of personality. At the same time, however, language also suggests that these traits are not totally separate. Many trait-names (good-natured, affable, amiable, cordial, friendly, genial, gentle, pleasant) are synonymous, and many others (good-natured versus peevish, lenient versus strict, friendly versus hostile, lovable versus hateful) are opposites.

Both the synonyms and antonyms just listed seem related to a general disposition that might be called agreeableness. The names of other traits (tidy, careful, responsible, scrupulous) and their opposites (messy, careless, irresponsible, unscrupulous) appear to be clusters of a subtraits in a different category—one that might be called conscientiousness.

Hierarchical Organization
In a classical study that looked at the details of such a structure, Norman (1963) asked participants to rate people they knew well on each of selected pairs of polar-opposite adjectives, and factor-analyzed the ratings. Factor analysis is a correlational procedure that assesses the degree to which people's responses to individual items, for example, on a test, correlate with one another but not with responses to other items. Those that go together are taken to reflect a separate underlying trait. For Norman's data, the ratings on the scales anchored by "talkative-silent," frank-secretive," and "sociable-reclusive" formed such a cluster, suggesting a basic trait of extroversion. The ratings on scales of "poised-tense," "composed-excitable," and "calm-anxious" formed another cluster, suggesting a separate trait of emotional stability that was independent of (did not correlate highly with) the trait of extroversion.

The full analysis of Norman's data revealed that five dimensions seemed to account for the correlations among the ratings: extroversion, later called "surgency"; agreeableness (friendliness, likability); conscientiousness (responsibility); emotional stability (absence of tension and anxiety); and culture, later called "quality of intellect" (curiosity, sensitivity, openness to experience). A host of more recent factor-analytic studies have come to a similar five-factor answer to the question, What are basic traits of personality? For that reason the literature calls these traits the "big five" (Goldberg 1993), and Zuckerman (1991, p. 17) refers to the general acceptance of this five-factor theory as the "Norman Conquest."

But the battle is not over. Some psychologists believe that the number of basic traits is more or fewer than five: Hans Eysenck (1964) proposed three, Raymond B. Cattell (1965) suggested sixteen, and other psychologists have offered other numbers. Such disagreement is possible because of problems that are inherent in the factor-analytic method. Factor-analytic statistics do not provide clear-cut criteria for identifying factors, especially when (as in the case of personality) traits appear to be nested: specific traits within general traits within supertraits. Additionally, the factor-analytic method leaves the naming of the factors up to the psychologists, who must decide which of the

40,000 trait names applies best to a factor: Is the right name "extroversion"; or should it be a noun form of "sociable," "friendly," "gregarious," "outgoing," "empathic," or "sympathetic"?

On the other hand, the factor-analytic methods can be applied in ways that deal with the first of these problems. Zuckerman reports one such application that has particular appeal because it puts 3-, 5-, and N-factor solutions into a single framework. Taking only minor liberties with the structure that Zuckerman (1991, p. 23) presents, it seems to me that his analyses suggest a structure consisting of three supertraits (positive emotionality, negative emotionality, and socialization), five general traits, and a less definite number (Zuckerman proposes seven) of specific traits. With the big five traits numbered to show how they function in this pattern, figure 7.3 depicts the structure.

The first supertrait, positive emotionality (PE in figure 7.3), brings together general traits of (1) social extroversion (EXT) and energy level (ENG). Social extroversion is also a specific trait, but energy level decomposes into speed of responding (SPD: liveliness, spirit) and forcefulness of responding (FCE: vigor, effectiveness). The second supertrait of negative emotionality (NE)—something like the big five's (2) emotional stability—is also a general trait made up of the specific traits of anger (ANG) and anxiety (ANX) The third supertrait of socialization (S) combines the general traits of impulsiveness (IMP) and openness to experience (OPE: the big five's (3) quality of intellect). Impulsiveness breaks down into inhibitory control (INH) and autonomy (AUT), which includes (4) conscientiousness but excludes conformity and lack of empathy. Openness of intellect is made up of experience (sensation) seeking (ES) and social desirability (SD), which resembles (5) agreeableness.

The Role of Context

Behavior that reflects the traits of personality displays something like the phenomenon of encoding specificity in memory. In a classical experiment that made essentially that point, Hartshorne and May (1928) studied deceitful behavior by observing children's cheating, lying, and stealing in the classroom and on the playground. They set up situations so that dishonesty would be possible but not inevitable. The chief finding of this study was that deceitful behavior is situation specific. For example, a child who cheated on one exam may cheat on another exam but not in a game with friends.

A great deal of research since then has shown that situations and personal dispositions interact in the production of behavior, although some situations are so powerful that almost everyone responds in the same way and some individual have traits so strong that they respond

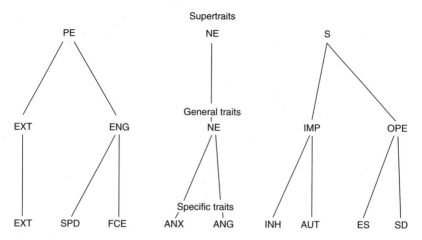

Figure 7.3
The Organization of Personality
This structure consists of three supertraits: positive emotionality (PE), negative emotionality (NE), and socialization (S). The supertraits bring together five general traits: social extroversion (EXT), energy level (ENG), negative emotionality (NE), impulsiveness (IMP), and openness to experience (OPE). Finally, nine specific traits are subordinate to the general traits: social extroversion (EXT), speed of reaction (SPD), forcefulness of reaction (FCE), anxiety (ANX), anger (ANG), inhibition (INH), autonomy (AUT), experience (sensation) seeking (ES), and social desirability (SD). The fact that negative emotionality and social extroversion appear at two levels is a result of the factor-analytic method. (Based on Zuckerman 1991.)

the same way in every situation. A situation in which there is a hoodlum with a switchblade knife makes almost everybody nervous and want to get away, but a few people have a need for the preservation of personal integrity so powerful that they would stand and fight the hoodlum. And some children have such a commitment to honesty that they would never cheat in any situation. But most of us are brave or honest under certain circumstances and cowardly or deceitful in others. The literature calls this situational specificity of traits a "trait-by-situation interaction." The environment (instigation) and personal dispositions (potential) both contribute to the etiology of behavior but in different proportions under different circumstances.

The Orthogenetic Principle

The organization of behavior and experience come about as a result of a process like Heinz Werner's (1957) orthogenetic principle, which holds that development proceeds from global mass reactions, through increasing differentiation, toward hierarchical organization of the differentiated units. The development of motor abilities, cognition, and personality follows such a pattern.

Physical Maturation
In his classic series of experiments on the development of locomotion in salamanders, Coghill (1929) showed that such development proceeds in orthogenetic stages. The first responses of the salamander tadpole to stimulation are global reactions of the organism's entire body. Later, this undifferentiated behavior gives way to more specific movements that appear first in the parts of the body near the tadpole's head and move downward toward the tail. With the development of limbs and land-going locomotion, the salamander gains control of its legs in a manner that begins with control of the joints near the central axis of the body, and moves to those that are more remote. Still later, these specific movements are coordinated into organized activity. Shirley's (1931) studies of the development of walking and Halverson's (1931) on grasping in human children both reveal the mass action-differentiation, cephalocaudal, and proximodistal sequences followed by coordinated action.

Cognitive Development
In the case of cognitive development, William James described the beginning of the orthogenetic pattern in his well-known statement, "The baby, assailed by eye, ears, nose, skin, and entrails at once, feels it all as one great blooming, buzzing confusion" (James 1890a, 1:488). Two of the most striking phenomena of early development, eidetic imagery and synesthesia, show that children retain some of this undifferentiated perceptual reaction for at least the first few years of life. A child who has eidetic imagery can still "see" a picture "out in space" or "on a screen in my head" after looking at that picture in a book. One with synesthesia experiences stimuli presented to one sensory system in terms of those normally produced by another: the smell of grapes is "purple"; the printed number 4 is "green"; the sound of the chimes of a clock is a "gold and silver striking of the hour." Both of these phenomena appear to be products of an undifferentiated cognitive system. The eidetiker does not distinguish between perception and memory. The child with synesthesia merges the data coming from one sensory modality with those that come from others.

In scattered sections of *Principles of Psychology*, in his treatment of the development of space perception, James described the entire orthogenetic principle: "The first fact that appears is that *primitively our space experiences form a chaos, out of which we have no immediate faculty for extri-*

cating them (James 1890a, 2:181). This fact raises a question: *"How do we* ARRANGE *these at first chaotically given spaces into the one regular and orderly 'world of space' which we now know?"* (2:146). The answer is that "subdivisions, once discriminated, acquire definite relations of position towards each other within the total space" (2:268). Then, *"The bringing of subdivisions to consciousness constitutes the entire process by which we pass from our first vague feeling of total vastness to a cognition of vastness in detail"* (2:152).

The results of more recent studies of the development of object perception also fit the orthogenetic pattern nicely. The youngest children see a picture of a bird made up of vegetables and fruits as an undifferentiated whole. Somewhat later it becomes an assemblage of disconnected parts. It is not until age seven that children perceive the integrated whole that is a bird (Elkind, Koegler, and Koegler 1964).

Personality Development

The organization of personality develops on a similar schedule. Global emotional reactions give way to increasingly specific traits and, with age, increasing integration. Several early theorists described such patterns. Bridges's (1932) account of the maturation of affect shows emotional development proceeding from diffuse excitement to more and more specific and then organized emotional reactions.

In psychoanalytic theory, the Freudian concept of primary process and the associated pleasure principle imply that children (and adults when they regress to autistic thinking) confuse reality with wishes, just as those with synesthesia confuse information coming from the different senses and those with eidetic imagery confuse memory with perceptual data. This undifferentiated reaction disappears with age and with the mastery of the reality principle, which requires a sharp distinction between the self and the environment. Later, the achievement of maturity requires an integration of the conflicting urges of the battling components of personality: superego, ego, and id.

The "person" (P) in Kurt Lewin's formula $B = f(P,E)$, presented on page 47, is an entity with both structural and dynamic properties (Lewin 1935). The fundamental structural concepts are intrapersonal regions (tendencies to act in the service of specific needs) separated from other regions by more or less permeable boundaries. The fundamental dynamic concepts are tensions that occur in appropriate regions with the arousal of a need and spread to other regions, putting them in tension, to the extent that the permeability of boundaries permits. With development, according to this theory, the number of regions in the person increases (differentiation), and the boundaries between regions become more permeable. This increased permeability gives the tensions in the most central regions access to other regions and in effect brings organization to the person.

Automaticity

Some organizations of behavior are automatic and involuntary. They proceed without attention and free the mind to deal with more important problems. Without thinking about what you are doing, you make breakfast and wonder what is happening with a friend who, for some reason, seems to have turned against you. You put your car on automatic pilot and drive from home to school or work, making plans along the way for how you will spend the day there. Later, reversals of such automatic habits take you home to dinner, while you mull over the successes and the failures of the past few hours. There is also experimental evidence for automatic habits. Without intention to recall such facts, students know automatically that the professor presented a certain bit of information twice in yesterday's lecture, at the beginning and toward the end, and that related information appears in the lower right-hand quarter of a page in the textbook. Apparently the temporal, spatial, and frequency attributes of messages are among those that have access to automatic processing (Hasher and Zachs 1979).

Levels of Organization

James believed that the brain is organized in levels and that the lower levels are the organs of our automatic habits: "We all of us have a definite routine manner of performing certain daily offices connected with the toilet, with the opening and shutting of familiar cupboards, and the like. Our lower centres know the order of these movements, and show their knowledge by their 'surprise' if the objects are altered so as to oblige the movements to be made in a different way. But our higher thought-centres know hardly anything about the matter. Few men can tell off-hand which sock, shoe or trouser-leg they put on first. . . . In action grown habitual, what instigates each new muscular contraction to take place in its appointed order is not a thought or a perception, but the *sensation occasioned by the muscular contraction just finished*" (James 1890a, 1:115).

Native Organizations   James's assignment of automatic habits to the lower brain suggests that some of them may be inborn. Sechenov, before him, took the stronger position that even the acts that we call voluntary are based on innate reflexes. The only capabilities of the neonate are a sensibility to stimulation and a repertoire of reflexes that are elicited en masse by appropriate stimuli. In the case of vision, for example, the infant has a tendency to be attracted to brightly colored objects. When such an object enters the visual field, the baby, reflexly, will keep that stimulus in view. "[T]he child will strive to keep the eyes in the position that gives the most pleasant sensation," which leads reflexly to a "widely irradiated set of muscular movements. The baby "screams, laughs, moves its arms, legs and body" (Sechenov 1935, pp. 293–294).

Stimuli and responses that occur together are associated and are easily shifted from one stimulus to another. The passion evoked in children by colored objects transfers successively to colored pictures of a knight in a story book, to the experience (or imagination) of themselves in the bright clothing of a knight, to the behavior of oneself as knight, and finally to the abstract attributes of knightly action—bravery, love of truth, human sympathy, self-restraint, and maturity of judgment. Thus, what began as the uncoordinated reflex reaction of the infant to brightly colored objects evolves into a sense of personal worth. The evolution of perception, memory, volition, thought, even moral values, is an evolution of reflexes—nothing more.

Overlearning   Probably most automatic habits—putting on your shoes and trousers, reading, writing, playing a musical instrument, swinging a golf club, driving a car—become automatic only with extended practice. Originally they required deliberation and attention. In James's terms, before these acts became automatic, they must have been functions of the higher centers of the brain that are the seat of consciousness (James 1890a, 1:66): "No animal without [these higher centers] can deliberate, pause, postpone, nicely weigh one motive against another, or compare. Prudence, in a word, is for such a creature, an impossible virtue. Accordingly we see that nature removes those functions in the exercise of which prudence is a virtue from the lower centres and hands them over to the cerebrum" (1: 21).

Adaptive and Occasional Maladaptive Value
By and large automatic habits are advantageous. In the words of William James, "Habit is thus the enormous fly-wheel of society, its most precious conservative agent. It alone is what keeps us all within the bounds of ordinance, and saves the children of fortune from the envious uprisings of the poor. It alone prevents the hardest and most repulsive walks of life from being deserted by those brought up to tread therein. . . . It dooms us all to fight out the battle of life upon the lines of our nature or our early choice, and to make the best of a pursuit that disagrees, because there is no other for which we are fitted, and it is too late to begin again. . . . It is well for the world that in most of

us, by age thirty, the character has set like plaster, and will never soften again" (James 1890a, 1:121).

Sometimes, however, automatized behavior works against you, chiefly when it leads you to neglect the world around you. Driving automatically, you run a stop sign and cause an accident. The processes that lead to such mishaps are the topic of the discussion that I turn to now.

When the Mechanism Fails

In the world of everyday activity, the organization of behavior involves an elaborate interaction among a host of excitatory and inhibitory processes. Stimuli potentiate, not just a single possible reaction but a population of candidates for action, of which only some are suited to the situation. As James suggested, the selection of appropriate behavior in such situations creates a problem for which inhibition is the solution. Acting on their energized potentials, people are as likely to do the crazy as the sane thing at any given moment. These possible performances are like dice thrown on a table. Unless the dice are loaded, what chance is there that the highest number will turn up oftener than the lowest? For adaptive behavior, loading the dice would mean bringing more or less constant pressure to bear in favor of those performances that serve best the interests of the individual. It would mean a constant inhibition of the tendencies to stray aside. Well, just such pressure and such inhibition are what consciousness seems to be exerting all the while (James 1890a, 1:140).

Two Varieties of Failure

In practice, this mechanism is usually successful. Inhibition puts the inappropriate responses out of action before they can occur. But sometimes things go wrong, in two different ways and in a variety of contexts.

First, because of long practice or high motivation, the excitatory strength of maladaptive habits can be too strong for inhibition to control. A basketball player can concentrate so much on what he is doing that he fails to see and pass the ball to a teammate who has a wide-open shot. Functional fixedness may inhibit behavioral flexibility and prevent creative problem solving. The maladaptive responses of the hungry chicken in the *Umweg* experiment, mentioned in the previous chapter, is one example from the laboratory. Similarly, when rats on their way to food in the goal box in a complex maze fail to inhibit a turn into a cul-de-sac that leads in the general direction of the goal box, the result is an anticipatory error.

Other errors of the same type include false starts at a track meet, off-sides of linemen in a football game, false alarms in an experiment on signal detection, and the déjà vu experience in human memory. Inflexible and stereotypic thinking about other groups of people inhibits the appreciation of individual differences within races and is at the root of ethnic prejudice. Alcoholism, antisocial personality, and childhood hyperactivity all represent an impairment of the ability of the central nervous system to inhibit response tendencies (Gorenstein 1992, p. 102).

Second, and more often, weakened inhibition results in lower thresholds for competing actions, and people fail to curb responses that they normally repress. When such weakening of inhibition occurs in drunkenness, it sometimes leads to the overly candid statements about other people or situations that we call "in vino veritas." In the so-called sleeper effect of messages on attitudes, people respond positively to counterattitudinal propoganda because, with time, they forget its source, which was what initially led them to inhibit that reaction. Regression occurs when the inhibitory restraints acquired in growing up dissolve in frustration. In the cruelest case of all, humane behavior gives way to obediently harming others in response to the disinhibiting commands of a person in authority (Milgram 1965).

Slips of the Tongue
Theoretically, the most interesting examples of such inhibitory failures occur in language. Together with their context, the first few words of any verbal communication (whether spoken, heard, read, or written) initiate a bottom-up process that accomplishes two things. It activates a sentence plan and calls up many possible next words. The words expressed or recognized are those that take the message forward; those that fail that test are cognitively inhibited, unless plans go astray. The following fragments of hebephrenic word salad show what can happen then. The first is from Bleuler's classic treatise (1950): "Olive oil is an Arabian liquor-sauce which the Afghans, Moors and Moslems use in ostrich farming. The Indian plantain tree is the whiskey of the Parsees and Arabs. Barley, rice and sugar cane called artichoke, grow remarkably well in India. The Brahmins live in castes in Baluchistan. The Circassians occupy Manchuria and China. China is the Eldorado of the Pawnees" (p. 15).

These two additional scraps of speech were created by a female schizophrenic patient: "My mother's name was Bill—and coo? St. Valentine's Day is the start of the breedin' season of the birds. All buzzards can coo. I'd like to see it pronounced buzzards rightly. They work hard.

So do parakeets." Asked to identify the color of a gray-colored chip, she responded, "Looks like clay. Sounds like gray. Take you for a roll in the hay. Hay day. Mayday. Help. I need help" (Chaika 1985, pp. 30, 32).

Fractions of these utterances are locally coherent. Taken two or three words at a time, they make sense. It is also easy to detect the underlying theme that takes the utterance off the track. The second example makes this point most clearly: To "bill and coo" is to express affection: "Valentine's Day" is the day of love ("the breedin' season"), and parakeets are "love birds." The associations are understandable but disorganized.

The potential for such cognitive derailment is in all of us, and sometimes we all behave like schizophrenics. We commit slips of the tongue and see words in print that are not there. And sometimes, as Freud emphasized, these slips betray hidden needs. But normally higher-level sentence plans, guided by acceptable motives, exclude off-target associations.

Summary and Conclusions

Behavior, whether deliberate or automatic, is the planning and execution of movements controlled by mental representations that serve the role of overarching plans. When behavior involves sequences of reactions occurring over time, these plans, in some sense, are present at the moment the behavioral sequence begins (Lashley 1951). The skills required to create or understand a sentence are everyday examples (Miller, Galanter, and Pribram 1960). In sentence comprehension, the organization of the whole sentence is essential to its understanding. The very different meanings of the two sentences, "The star's brilliance illuminated the otherwise dull play" and "The star's brilliance illuminated the otherwise dull night," become clear only at the end. The discrete reactions to individual words in sentences depend on a theme; certainly words are not processed singly or consciously.

The fact of such organizations raises questions that challenge psychology's commitment to analysis: What are the elements and how do they achieve coherence? The answer to these questions is that the most basic elements are the sensory and neural processes, with which experience and behavior begin. But even at the level of the receptors, these rudimentary components interact, producing higher-order outcomes—in vision, edges, angles, lines in motion—that the brain treats as unitary. This pattern is the model on which more elaborate processing is fashioned. The elements of stimulation combine in bottom-up reactions to produce higher organizations that operate, top-down, to determine the nature of experience from then on.

In everyday existence, two additional facts are important: (1) The organizations combine to form hierarchies; such structures exist for cognition, affect, and reaction tendencies. (2) Contexts determine which of many available structures control behavior. The phenomenon of encoding specificity and trait-by-situation interactions is among the most studied of these effects of context.

The development of the organizations of reaction tendencies, cognition, and affect all occurs on a schedule that Heinz Werner called the orthogenetic principle. Development is from generality, to specificity, to organizations of the specifics. With long practice, such organizations become automatic, an outcome that is usually adaptive because it frees the mind to deal with important issues and emergencies. When the automatic mechanism fails, however, the result can be destructive. When attention pricks the bubble of automatized behavioral coherence, the result is often error. Everyone who plays a musical instrument knows that thinking about the details of a performance can spoil it. The "analysis paralysis" reported by talented athletes has led to more than one defeat in college sports, for example, when concentrating on component movements makes a player miss the field goal or the free throw that would win the game.

Chapter 8

Epilogue: To Give Psychology Away

The challenges that face the world today are monumental. In some places on the planet people are dying of starvation; elsewhere they are committing suicide with drugs, cholesterol, and unprotected sex. Divorce, desertion, dual careers, and teenage parenthood have eroded family structures; the major loyalties of many parents are outside the home; children are forgotten and neglected or abused. Some old people spend their last boring, hopeless days in nursing homes; others have no homes at all. The risks of murder, rape, and mugging make city streets unsafe to walk on; the celebration of aggression by the media numbs the horror of people's reactions to such violence. The values that different segments of society hold sacred are divided; some people worship the almighty dollar, while others glorify the tyranny of fundamentalist religion. The nation-states are constantly at one another's throats. Pollution seems determined to make the world unlivable. Bitter hatred marks relationships among diverse cultural groups.

The persistence of these miseries shows that the typical reactions of society to its troubles will never bring relief. New laws will not correct them because attitudes cannot be legislated. Moral indignation will not make them go away. Progress in medicine and engineering will not develop cures because they are not medical or engineering problems. They are problems of behavior and, thus, problems for psychology because psychology is the science of behavior.

In stronger terms, it can be argued that psychology has an obligation to use its knowledge in a search for the solutions to these problems. The discipline possesses whatever expertise it has because of previous support by the community. Thus, psychology is indebted to society, and, in the words of George Miller (1969), it has the responsibility to give itself away to serve the common good. The first step in our gift-giving program must be the education of the public, an effort that is hindered by misunderstanding of psychology by society and by misdirected actions of the discipline itself.

What the Public Is Nearly Ready to Accept

The previous chapters of this book suggest that psychology's gift to humanity is a present in two parts, some assembly required: a methodological component, the application to behavior of the rules of science described in chapters 1 and 2; and a substantive component, the principles of behavior described in chapters 3 through 7. The potential recipients of this gift may not appreciate the methodological portion because, applied to human conduct, science clashes with established habits of interpretation. The substantive part will be easier for the public to accept because the principles have been standard ways of thought since at least the time of Aristotle. Although this understanding needs fine-tuning, it is where public education about psychology might begin.

Potential versus Instigated Action

The distinction between potential and performance appears in the common understanding that there are innate potentials for the development of medical disorders; that children seldom perform up to the level of their ability; that diseases may be in remission, existing without symptoms; and that an addict who gives up a drug may never lose the habit.

After that auspicious beginning, however, common thinking goes astray. Applied to human accomplishment, it maintains that people use only 10 percent (or some other small fraction) of their brain power, although there is no limit to what they can accomplish if they labor hard enough. Indeed, some people work so hard that they become overachievers. No doubt the inconsistencies are obvious. The denominator in a fraction is a total; if people never use the total, that number, and thus the fraction, are both unknowable. If there is no limit to accomplishment, performance greater than one's limit of ability is a logical impossibility, and overachievement is an oxymoron.

Adaptation versus Coping

People understand that personal control (coping) is possible in certain situations, whereas the acceptance of reality (adaptation) is the only choice available in others. A slogan of Alcoholics Anonymous catches the sense of the distinction: "God grant me the serenity to accept [adapt to] the things I cannot change, the courage to change [cope with] those that I can, and the wisdom to know the difference." These forms of adjustment may even distinguish cultures. In his contrast between their relationships to nature, Tony Hillerman seems to say that Hopi Indians cope and Navahos adapt: "The Hopis held a rain dance

Sunday, calling on the clouds . . . to restore the water blessing to the land. [But it is] not a Navaho concept, this idea of adjusting nature to human needs. The Navaho adjusted himself to remain in harmony with the universe. When nature withheld the rain, the Navaho sought the pattern of this phenomenon—as he sought the pattern of all things—to find its beauty and live in harmony with it" (Hillerman 1978, p. 44).

Thresholds for Behavior
In ordinary life, the threshold concept is implicit in such questions as: Does this athlete have the talent required to make the team? Is that painting good enough to be in a juried show? Does this manuscript meet the criteria for acceptance by this journal? The threshold question is also at the heart of many social issues: Is abortion the murder of a human being or something less than that? Is a child with an IQ above 145 necessarily a genius? Is sexual intercourse that occurs when some-one seduces someone else whose senses are impaired by alcohol really rape?

Opponent-Process Theory
It is common knowledge that many life events are governed by oppo-nent processes, but people frequently misuse that understanding. Mis-applications of the concept have produced such fictions as the so-called law of averages, including the gambler's fallacy that a run of good luck will surely be followed by a run of bad luck; the notion that in mate selection opposites attract; and the hypothesis that there is a law of compensation in nature, whereby a person who is strong in one capac-ity will be weak in others (the stereotypes of the "stupid jock" and "cute dumb broad" are examples).

Hierarchical Organization and Context
People are familiar with a variety of hierarchical organizations. They know that some individuals are so obsessed with certain goals and ways of doing that their interactions with the world are inflexible and ineffective. Students realize that organized ideas are an aid to compre-hension, learning, and remembering. They use outlines and tree dia-grams as ways of organizing oral reports and term papers. Sentence diagrams, mathematical equations, and computer flowcharts describe the organizations of the structures to which they apply. The members of the groups affected know that the administrative structures of uni-versities and street gangs are organized and hierarchical.

People also understand the role of context as a determinant of be-havior and express it in their rules of conduct (when in Rome, do as the Romans do) and in the insight that the meaning of an action depends on the circumstances. As William James said somewhere, in a comment that I have been unable to recover, it is one thing to step on a man's toe and apologize but quite another to apologize and then step on his toe.

What the Public Is More Than Ready to Reject

Although a successful program of public education about psychology might build on these approximate beginnings, there is a major obstacle: an attitude toward psychology that is more than just a little negative.

William James had unkind things to say about both of psychology's two sciences. Speaking of experimental, he remarked, "This method taxes patience to the utmost, and could hardly have arisen in a country whose natives could be *bored*. Such Germans as Weber, Fechner, and Wundt obviously cannot" (James 1890a, 1:192). But, grudgingly, James also recognized the method's power: "There is little of the grand style in these prism, pendulum and chronograph philosophers. They mean business, not chivalry. What generous divination, and that superiority in virtue which was thought by Cicero to give a man the best insight into nature, have failed to do, their spying and scraping, their deadly tenacity and almost diabolical cunning, will doubtless someday bring about" (1:193)

In James's time, mental tests had not yet made their appearance in the Western world. About the only correlational methods in general use were questionnaires, and James did not like them, either: "Messrs Darwin and Galton have set the example of circulars of questions sent out by the hundreds to those supposed able to reply. The custom has spread, and it will be well for us in the next generation if such circulars not be ranked among the common pests of life" (James 1890a, 1:194).

Psychology's Image Problem

Something like James's negative evaluation is in the public mind today. Many people doubt that a science of psychology is possible or proper. They believe that certain qualities of human life, such as envy, awe, love, creativity, and wonder, cannot—and should not—be quantified or studied by objective methods. They feel that the methods and the knowledge of psychology are intrusive and coercive. Experiments and mental tests pry into matters that ought to be protected by the right to privacy. The idea that human conduct obeys natural laws seems as offensive as the regulations that force otherwise free people to observe speed limits and pay income taxes.

Paradoxically, along with their doubts about the feasibility of a science of psychology, people fear what they take to be the discipline's enormous power. Failing to distinguish betweenscience and pseudoscience, they think that the methods of psychology include mind reading, witchcraft, brainwashing, behavioral programming, and thought control. Misreading the purposes of science, they feel that psychologists use subliminal influence and other mysterious methods to "psych people out" in order to obtain a personal advantage through trickery that they otherwise could not.

The origins of such mistrust are in a discrepancy between common sense and science, in their positions on the hallmarks of the scientific method. Table 8.1 reviews the conflict. Of all the differences noted there, the one about the causes of behavior (determinism) is the greatest obstacle to public acceptance of psychology.

Table 8.1
Common Sense and the Hallmarks of Scientific Psychology

	Common Sense	Scientific Thinking
Empiricism	Dictionary definition	Operational definition
	What language tells us	What research tells us
	Meaning 3	Meanings 1 and 2
	Authority	Evidence
	Intuition	Observation
	Television and other media	Scientific literature
	Superstition	Experimental results
	What experience has taught me	Accumulated data
	Single cases	Large samples
	What everybody knows	What has been demonstrated
	What only stands to reason	Deductions from formal theory
Analysis	Nonanalytic	Analytic
	Whole persons	Attributes of individuals
	Total situations	Elements of stimulation
	Wholes are primary and give parts meaning	Organizations of parts create wholes
Determinism	Free will	Determinism
	Mental causes	Physical causes
	Single causes	Complex causality
	"Tell it like it is"	"More research is needed"
	Explanation by naming	Explanation by theory and law
	Dispositional explanation	Deductive explanation
	"The simple, unvarnished truth"	Probabilistic interpretation
	"Exceptions prove the rule"	Exceptions disprove the rule

Implicitly honoring the power of personal will, people view behavior as expressions of traits or dispositions that are the properties of individuals; they discount the influence of external causes. The social psychologists call this preference for dispositional explanations the *fundamental attribution error*. Thus, students believe they have the ability (one disposition) to master any subject if they have the persistence (another disposition) to study long and hard enough; they underestimate the importance of situational factors such as the difficulty of the subject, grading standards, and the quality of instruction. Teachers, in their turn, complain that students do less well in their courses than they ought to because they are uninvolved, dim-witted, or lazy; they neglect the possibility that the textbook and their lectures are a bore and the assignments pure drudgery.

The fundamental attribution error generalizes to populations, creating the stereotypes that attribute universal traits to groups of people, sometimes to excuse discrimination. You know the worst offenders: "Women don't go into science because they have no aptitude for mathematics"; "blacks end up in professional athletics instead of academics because they are strong of body, weak of mind."

The preference for dispositional causality even appears in the pseudopsychological explanations that people have for events outside the realm of animal behavior. The weather, the stock market, Lady Luck, and the weeds in the garden all do what they do because they have "minds of their own." Science long ago gave up the habit of treating resident properties as causes, but the practice is alive and well in common ways of thinking—and, unfortunately, in some branches of psychology.

Chaos in Psychology and Its Consequences

If psychology is to contribute to solutions of the problems of the world, it must find ways to make the public see the advantages of scientific interpretations over those discussed above. Before it can succeed in that campaign, however, it must solve some problems of its own. Contemporary psychology is a discipline divided. Psychologists live in quarrelsome cultures whose interactions are determined more by temperament than reason (Kimble 1984). The knowledge of psychology is an array of bits and pieces. Instead of any organizing theme, we have a byzantine array of what the introductory textbooks call "perspectives"—behavioristic, biological, cognitive, developmental, experimental, functional, Gestalt, holistic, humanistic, personalistic, psychodynamic, psychometric, sociocultural, transactional (and no doubt some that I have repressed) all of them, as a politically correct philosophy requires, created equal.

These differences define the fault lines along which psychological associations and university departments have shattered; they make it difficult for psychology so speak about the problems of the world with other than a forked tongue. One way to organize a presentation of the details of all this foolishness is in terms of Aristotle's triarchic view of human talent.

Cognition

Some of the problems of psychology are the same as those that frustrate public understanding, and for the same reason. The language of psychology is also that of common sense. Language is the agent of cognition, the currency of thinking, the toolbox of communication and the custodian of culture. To be useful, it must map onto the world with some precision. Unfortunately, the fact that it does so encourages the faith that the fit is perfect and that truth is in the dictionary. If there is a word for it, there must be a corresponding item of reality. If there are two words, there must be two realities and they must be different. The classical mind-body problem is a venerable example of this delusion. That whole dreary history is the record of a search for entities and interactions that are taken to exist for no better reason than the fact that people talk as though they do.

James recognized the problem: "Whenever we have made a word ... to denote a certain group of phenomena, we are prone to suppose a substantive entity existing beyond the phenomena. [And] the *lack* of a word quite often leads to the opposite error. We are then prone to suppose that no entity can be there; and so we overlook phenomena whose existence would be patent to us all, had we only grown up to hear it familiarly recognized in speech" (James 1890a, 1:195).

In psychology more recently, this fallacy has created more than just a little mischief. It encouraged psychologists to believe that they had altered something factual when they changed the names of "instinct" to "drive," "free will" to "intrinsic motivation," "neurosis" to "personality disorder," and "feeblemindedness," first to "mental retardation" and then to "cognitive challenge." Some versions of the most fashionable perspectives in psychology today (cognitive, biological, and holistic) have disabling defects deriving from the same assumption.

Cognitive Psychology's Phantom Information Processor

Consider, for example, the fantasy that there is a little person named cognition—sometimes, to make it worse, inside the head—who is busily processing information, retrieving memories, making plans, creating schemata, and parsing text. In approximately the words of E. B. Holt (1931, p. 254), in such theorizing, bits of information go straight

to the pineal gland, where they become cognitions that serve the pleasure and instruction of the homunculus residing there. After he en-
codes the information, the homunculus, if so inclined, may initiate and
execute responses. In the pineal gland the charivari of mind goes on, a
"veritable tumbling ground for whimsies" (the phrase is from William
James 1890a, 1:163). No doubt you detect the presence of Descartes in
Holt's bit of whimsy and realize that, for "cognition," you could substi-
tute "the soul" without damage to the science.

Biological Psychology's Ghost in the Machine

The behaviorists have always given physiology a subsidiary role in the
science of psychology. Watson (1913) thought of anatomy and physiology as handmaidens to psychology. He believed that psychological
knowledge would dictate the form that the laws of these sciences
would have to take. Throughout his long career, B. F. Skinner was pro-
vocatively antiphysiological, announcing in 1938 that "the gain to the
science of behavior from neurological hypotheses in the past is, I believe, quite certainly outweighed by all the misdirected experimenta-
tion and bootless theorizing that have arisen from the same source"
(p. 426). Half a century later (1990), he advised psychology to treat
physiological reactions as responses, just another class of things that
organisms do.

   This cheapening of the value of physiology troubles some psychologists, who feel that the behaviorists' "empty organism" or "black box"
should be filled with something tangible and real. Instead of stimulus-
response psychology, they call for a stimulus-organism-response psychology that makes behavior the result of material causes that are
primarily in the nervous system. Innocent as it may seem, that conception presents psychologists with a temptation—and some of them
have yielded—to commit two deadly sins. The second sin is sloth, a
lazy contentment with a physiology that has no relation to behavior.
The first sin is false pride, the presumption that explanations that in-
voke the religious authority of the nervous system are more explanatory than others because only they are real. In actuality, until its
functions are related to behavior, the nervous system is just the house
in which the cognitive psychologists' ghost-soul lives.

Holistic Hypostatization

Some of the advocates of holism have noted that established sciences
treat important phenomena as wholes, and they suggest that, for ad-
vancement as a science, psychology must do likewise. It is true, for
example, that astronomy deals with the solar system as a totality, by
sets of equations that describe the interactions among the variables

that control the system's parts. Moreover, some minitheories in psychology are similar. Korte's (1915) theory of the phi phenomenon, Gestalt psychology's prototypical whole, was an early example. Korte set forth three laws that stated the interactions among intensity, temporal separation, and the spatial distance of two stimuli that produce optimal apparent motion.

One could hope that such theorizing is what the holistically inclined psychologists have in mind when they argue for a psychology of totalities. That is not the case at all, however. These psychologists imagine that the whole is somehow different from and greater than its parts. The whole gives meaning to the parts and is in charge of them. These fantasies reify the whole and make it worthy of a name, like "whole child" or "total personality." Now this baptized agency does things and owns things. It knows itself, or if it does not, it finds itself and seeks self-actualization. It has personal freedom and human dignity; a self-concept and assorted different selves; internal locus of control and out-of-body experiences. This orgy of hypostatization—the assumption that abstract concepts are physical things with mandated names—creates a voodoo psychology that mistakes spirit words for explanations.

Affect and Reaction Tendency

These ill-advised opinions gained acceptance in some quarters with the revolt against the positivistic science of psychology early in the second half of the twentieth century. The most unattractive aspect of that revolution was (and is) the corruption of scholarship by politically inspired assaults on truth. Putting more faith in their autistic notions of what ought to be than scientific evidence of what is, the devotees of political correctness commit a moralistic fallacy. When the outcomes of research appear to violate their values, they insist that the results cannot be true. They have dismissed studies of obedience, the life expectancies of left-handed people, and race differences in IQ on the basis of such biases. And in their scorn for science, they fail to realize that facts cannot be established by the method of proclamation or that how they feel about a finding has no bearing on its truth.

The politically correct attitude is deficient in cognition. It is mindless affect made manifest in mindless doing. In the colleges and universities, the champions of political correctness advocate an antiacademic curriculum that emphasizes feeling over information, intuition over evidence, and moral right and wrong over intellectual right and wrong. They promote the appreciation of diversity instead of skills and knowledge as the goal of education. They dishonor teaching by

turning instruction into touchy-feely therapy, where the students' attitudes, announced in consciousness-raising psychobabble, are as highly
valued as anything the professors or the textbooks have to offer.

The leaders of this anti-intellectual crusade treat the evils in the
world as targets of condemnation rather than as issues to be understood. Their interest in fixing problems is distinctly secondary to their
urge to fix the blame. When it comes to social action, they take stands
and sometimes establish programs, unencumbered by a need for evidence. Politics instead of science have dictated their positions on abortion, affirmative action, gun control, bans on certain advertising,
whether tests are biased against women and the members of certain
minority groups, and whether homosexuality and shyness are mental
illness.

These positions and the campaigns to which they lead are surely
well intended, but they are not the stuff that rational solutions to the
problems of humankind are made of. Quoting William James one final
time, "With mere good intentions, the road to hell is proverbially
paved" (James 1890a, 1:125).

Summary and Conclusion: The Hope of Application

As everybody says today, the world is going to hell in a handbasket.
The problems that bedevil it are mainly behavioral, and eventually
the knowledge of psychology will be the key to their solution. What
psychology has to offer for this purpose is a scientific understanding
of behavior; applications exploit the science of psychology and draw
their strength from it. A key component in psychology's program to
give itself away must be to educate the public about the science of
psychology.

That task will not be easy. Although people routinely think in terms
of the hypotheses about behavior that this book identifies as fundamental, applied to human conduct, the scientific methods that lie behind these principles clash with established ways of thought. Probably
it is the mistrust that grows out of this conflict of scientific sense and
common sense that leads many people to regard a science of psychology as intrusive and coercive—and, fortunately, impossible.

Contemporary psychology is ill prepared to deal with its image
problem, for two reasons. There is very little coherence in its subject
matter, and too frequently the supporters of its popular perspectives
violate the rules of science. Many of the cognitive psychologists have
disowned empiricism and appointed mythical mental managers to
oversee the business of the mind, failing to understand that processes
without overt expression are beyond the reach of science. Some of the

biological psychologists have such an obsession with the machinery of the body that they neglect behavior, failing to understand that mechanisms without behavioral expression are not the business of psychology. In reckless celebration of the psychologist's fallacy, the holists have mounted a campaign against analysis, failing to understand that a nonanalyzing science is an inarticulate science.

A particularly difficult internal problem that confronts psychology when it turns to application is a mindless preference for "politically correct" remedies, based on social science reflexes, which render science irrelevant to advocacy. But if psychology is to help in conquering the problems of the world, it must stick to its scientific guns. It must make its contribution in the honest coin of scientific knowledge, not the phony currency of politically correct affect.

Moreover, direct social advocacy is beyond the limits of the discipline's authority. Immediate responsibility for the application of psychology belongs not to psychology itself but to other agencies. To protect its integrity as a science, psychology must refrain from direct social action and restrict itself to providing those other agencies with knowledge that will help them make wise decisions.

References

Andreasen, N. C. (1985). Positive vs. negative schizophrenia: A critical evaluation. *Schizophrenia, 11,* 380–389.

Behrman, M., Moscovitch, M., and Winocur, G. (1994). Mental imagery without visual perception of objects: Evidence from a patient with visual agnosia. *Journal of Experimental Psychology: Human Perception and Performance, 20,* 1068–1087.

Bleuler, E. (1950). *Dementia praecox or the group of schizophrenias.* New York: International Universities Press.

Bousfield, W. A. (1953). The occurrence of clustering in the free recall of randomly arranged associates. *Journal of General Psychology, 49,* 229–240.

Bower, G. H., Monteiro, K. P., and Gilligan, S. G. (1978). Emotional mood as a context for learning and recall. *Journal of Verbal Learning and Verbal Behavior, 17,* 573–585.

Breland, K., and Breland, M. (1961). The misbehavior of organisms. *American Psychologist, 16,* 681–684.

Bridges, K. M. B. (1932). Emotional development in early infancy. *Child Development, 3,* 324–341.

Bridgman, P. W. (1938). *The logic of modern physics.* New York: Macmillan.

Bruner, J. S. (1968). Processes of cognitive growth: Infancy. *Eighth Annual Report of the Harvard Center for Cognitive Studies.* Cambridge: Harvard University Press.

Cajori, F. (ed.). (1947). *Sir Isaac Newton's mathematical principles of natural philosophy and his system of the world.* Berkeley: University of California Press.

Carroll, L. (1954). *Through the looking-glass.* New York: Dutton. (First published 1871).

Cattell, R. B. (1965). *The scientific analysis of personality.* Chicago: Aldine.

Chaika, E. (1985). Crazy talk. *Psychology Today, 19,* 30–35.

Chase, W. G., and Simon, H. A. (1973). Perception in chess. *Cognitive Psychology, 4,* 55–81.

Cofer, C. N., and Appley, M. H. (1964). *Motivation: Theory and research.* New York: Wiley.

Coghill, C. E. (1929). *Anatomy and the problem of behavior.* New York: Macmillan.

Cronbach, L. J. (1957). The two disciplines of scientific psychology. *American Psychologist, 12,* 671–684.

Dahlstrom, W. G. (1985). The development of psychological testing. In G. A. Kimble and K. Schlesinger (eds.), *Topics in the history of psychology.* Hillsdale, N.J.: Lawrence Erlbaum Associates.

Dawes, R. M, Faust, D., and Meehl, P. E. (1989). Clinical versus actuarial judgment. *Science, 243,* 1668–1673.

Dollard, J., and Miller, N. E. (1950). *Personality and psychotherapy: An analysis in terms of learning, thinking, and culture.* New York: McGraw-Hill.

Dweck, C. S., and Repucci, N. D. (1973). Learned helplessness and reinforcement responsibility in children. *Journal of Personality and Social Psychology, 25,* 109–116.

Elkind, D., Koegler, R. R., and Koegler, E. G. (1964). Studies in perceptual development: II. Part-whole perception. *Child Development, 35,* 81–90.

Ericsson, K. A., Chase, W. G., and Faloon, S. (1980). Acquisition of a memory skill. *Science, 208,* 1181–1182.

Eysenck, H. J. (1964). Principles and methods of personality descriptions, classification and diagnosis. *British Journal of Psychology, 55,* 284–294.

Gilbert, D. T., Krull, D. S., and Malone, P. (1990). Unbelieving the unbelievable: Some problems in the rejection of false information. *Journal of Personality and Social Psychology, 59,* 601–603.

Gleick, J. (1987). *Chaos: Making a new science.* New York: Penguin Books.

Goldberg, L. R. (1993). The structure of phenotypic personality. *American Psychologist, 48,* 267–234.

Goleman, D. (1985). *Vital lies, simple truths.* New York: Simon and Schuster.

Gorenstein, E. E. (1992). *The science of mental illness.* New York: Academic Press.

Hanfmann, E., and Kasanin, J. (1937). A method for the study of concept formation. *Journal of Psychology, 3,* 521–540.

Hartshorne, H., and May, M. A. (1928). *Studies in deceit.* New York: Macmillan.

Halverson, A. M. (1931). An experimental study of prehension in infants by means of systematic cinema records. *General Psychology Monographs, 10,* 2–3.

Hasher, L. (1994). Inhibition and cognition. Paper presented at the Annual Meeting of the American Psychological Society, Washington, D.C.

Hasher, L., and Zacks, R. T. (1979). Automatic and effortful processing in memory. *Journal of Experimental Psychology: General, 108,* 356–388.

Hernandez-Peon, R., Scherer, H., and Jouvet, M. (1956). Modifications of electrical activity in cochlear nucleus during "attention" in unanesthetized cats. *Science, 123,* 331–332.

Hilgard, E. R., and Marquis, D. G. (1940). *Conditioning and learning.* New York: Appleton-Century-Crofts.

Hillerman, T. (1978). *The listening woman.* New York: Harper Collins.

Holt, E. B. (1931). *Animal drive and the learning process.* New York: Henry Holt.

Horowitz, M. J. (1986). *Stress response syndromes.* 2d ed. Northvale, N.J.: Jason Aronson.

Hovland, C. I. (1937). The generalization of conditioned responses: I. The sensory generalization of conditioned responses with varying frequencies of tone. *Journal of General Psychology, 17,* 125–148.

Hubel, D. H., and Wiesel, T. N. (1959). Receptor fields of single neurons in the cat's striate cortex. *Journal of Physiology, 148,* 574–591.

Hull, C. L. (1929). A functional interpretation of the conditioned reflex. *Psychological Review, 36,* 498–511.

Hull, C. L. (1943). *Principles of behavior.* New York: D. Appleton-Century.

Hurvich, L. M., and Jameson, D. (1957). An opponent process theory of color vision. *Psychological Review, 64,* 384–404.

James, W. (1887). Reflex action and theism. In W. James (ed.), *The will to believe.* New York: Longmans Green.

James, W. (1890a). *The principles of psychology.* New York: Henry Holt.

James, W. (1890b). The importance of individuals. *Open Court, 4,* 437–440.

James, W. (1893). *Psychology.* New York: Holt.

Killeen, P. R. (1989). Behavior as a trajectory through a field of attractors. In J. R. Brink and C. R. Haden (eds.), *The computer and the brain: Perspectives on human artificial intelligence.* The Hague: Elsevier Science Publishers (North-Holland).

Kimble, G. A. (1953). Psychology as a science. *Scientific Monthly, 77,* 156–160.

Kimble, G. A. (1956). *Principles of general psychology.* New York: Ronald Press.

Kimble, G. A. (1971). Attitudinal factors in eyelid conditioning. In G. A. Kimble (ed.), *Foundations of conditioning and learning.* New York: Appleton-Century-Crofts.

Kimble, G. A. (1984). Psychology's two cultures. *American Psychologist, 39,* 833–839.

Kimble, G. A. (1985). Conditioning and learning. In G. A. Kimble and K. Schlesinger (eds.), *Topics in the history of psychology.* Hillsdale, N.J.: Lawrence Erlbaum Associates.

Kimble, G. A. (1989). Psychology from the standpoint of a generalist. *American Psychologist, 44,* 491–499.

Kimble, G. A. (1990a). Mother Nature's bag of tricks is small. *Psychological Science, 1,* 36–41.

Kimble, G. A. (1990b). To be or ought to be? That is the question. *American Psychologist, 45,* 558–560.

Kimble, G. A. (1993). A modest proposal for a minor revolution in the language of psychology. *Psychological Science, 4,* 253–255.

Kimble, G. A., and Ost, J. W. P. (1961). A conditioned inhibitory process in eyelid conditioning. *Journal of Experimental Psychology, 61,* 150–156.

Kimble, G. A., and Perlmuter, L. (1970). The problem of volition. *Psychological Review, 77,* 361–384.

Kintsch, W. (1994). Text comprehension, memory, and learning. *American Psychologist, 49,* 294–303.

Koch, S. (1993). "Psychology" or "the psychological studies"? *American Psychologist, 48,* 902–904.

Konorski, J. (1948). *Conditioned reflexes and neuron organization.* Cambridge: Cambridge University Press.

Konorski, J. (1960). The cortical "representation" of unconditioned reflexes. *International Journal of Electroencephalography and Clinical Neurophysiology, 13* (Suppl.), 81–90.

Korte, A. (1915). Kinematoscopische Untersuchungen. *Zeitschrift für Psychologie, 72,* 193–206.

Langer, E., and Rodin, J. (1976). The effects of choice and enhanced personal responsibility for the aged: A field experiment in an institutional setting. *Journal of Personality and Social Psychology, 34,* 191–198.

Lashley, K. S. (1951). The problem of serial order in behavior. In L. A. Jeffress (ed.), *Cerebral mechanisms in behavior: The Hixon Symposium* (pp. 112–146). New York: Wiley.

Lewin, K. (1935). *A dynamic theory of personality.* New York: McGraw-Hill.

Lewin, K. (1938). *Contributions to psychological theory: The conceptual representation and the measurement of psychological forces.* Durham, N.C.: Duke University Press.

Little, K., and Schneidman, E. S. (1959). Congruences among interpretations of psychological tests and anamnestic data. *Psychological Monographs, 73* (Whole No. 476).

Locke, J. (1964). *An essay concerning human understanding.* New York: Meridian (originally published in 1690).

Luchins, A. S. (1942). Mechanization in problem-solving: The effect of Einstellung. *Psychological Monographs, 54* (Whole No. 248).

Maier, S. F., and Seligman, M. E. P. (1976). Learned helplessness: Theory and evidence. *Journal of Experimental Psychology: General, 105,* 3–46.

Maslow, A. H. (1970). *Motivation and personality* (2d ed.). New York: Harper & Row.

Maxwell, J. C. (1882). Science and free will. Reprinted in L. Campbell, and W. Garnett (eds.), *The life of James Clerk Maxwell.* Westport, Conn.: Johnson Reprint Corp., 1969.

Michotte, A. (1963). *The perception of causality.* Paterson, N.J.: Littlefield.

Milgram, S. (1965). Some conditions of obedience to authority. *Human Relations, 18,* 56–76.

Miller, G. A. (1969). Psychology as a means of promoting human welfare. *American Psychologist, 24,* 1063–1075.

Miller, G. A., Galanter, E., and Pribram, K. H. (1960). *Plans and the structure of behavior.* New York: Holt, Rinehart and Winston.

Miller, J. G. (1941). *Unconscious.* New York: Wiley.

Mowrer, O. H. (1960). *Learning theory and behavior.* New York: Wiley.

Myers, I. B. (1962). *Manual: The Myers-Briggs Type Indicator.* Princeton, N.J.: Educational Testing Service.

Norman, W. T. (1963). Toward an adequate taxonomy of personality attributed: Replicated factor structure in peer nomination personality ratings. *Journal of Abnormal and Social Psychology.* 66, 574–583.

Pavlov, I. *Conditioned reflexes.* Oxford: Oxford University Press, 1927.

Peirce, C. S., and Jastrow, J. (1884). On small differences in perception. *Memoirs of the National Academy of Sciences, 3,* 75–83.

Piaget, J. (1930). *The child's conception of physical causality.* New York: Harcourt.

Piaget, J. (1952). Autobiography. In E. G. Boring (ed.), *A history of psychology in autobiography,* Vol. 4. Worcester, Mass.: Clark University Press.

Pratt, C. C. (1939). *The logic of modern psychology.* New York: Macmillan.

Rescorla, R. A. (1967). Pavlovian conditioning and its proper control procedures. *Psychological Review, 74,* 71–80.

Rodin, J. (1986). Aging and health: Effects of the sense of control. *Science, 223,* 1271–1276.

Rorschach, H. (1921). *Psychodiagnostik.* Bern, Switzerland: Huber.

Ross, T. A. (1937). *The common neuroses.* Baltimore: William Wood & Co.

Rozin, P., Haidt, J., and McCauley, C. R. (1994). Disgust. In M. Lewis and J. Haviland (eds.), *Handbook of emotions.* New York: Guilford.

Rumelhart, D. E., McClelland, J. L., and the PDP Research Group (1986). Parallel distributed processing: Explorations in the microstructure of cognition. In J. A. Feldman, P. J. Hayes, and D. E. Rumelhart (eds.), *Computational models of cognition and perception.* Cambridge, Mass.: MIT Press.

Sechenov, I. M. (1935). *Selected works.* Moscow: State Publishing House (originally published in 1860).

Selye, H. (1976). *The stress of life* (rev. ed.). New York: McGraw-Hill.

Sheldon, W. H. (1942). *The varieties of temperament: A psychology of constitutional differences.* New York: Harper & Rowe 1942.

Sherrington, C. S. (1906). *The integrative action of the nervous system.* London: Constable & Co.

Shirley, M. M. (1931). *The first two years of life: A study of twenty-five babies,* Vol. 1. Minneapolis: University of Minnesota Press.

Siegel, S. (1979). The role of conditioning in drug tolerance and addiction. In J. D. Keehn (ed.), *Psychopathology in animals: Research and treatment implications.* New York: Academic Press.

Siegel, S. (1984). Pavlovian conditioning and heroin overdose. *Bulletin of the Psychonomic Society, 22,* 428–430.

Skinner, B. F. (1938). *The behavior of organisms: An experimental analysis.* New York: D. Appleton-Century.

Skinner, B. F. (1948). Superstition in the pigeon. *Journal of Experimental Psychology, 38,* 168–172.

Skinner, B. F. (1957). *Verbal behavior.* Englewood Cliffs, N.J.: Prentice-Hall.

Skinner, B. F. (1971). *Beyond freedom and dignity.* New York: Knopf.

Skinner, B. F. (1990). Can there be a science of mind? *American Psychologist, 45,* 1206–1210.

Solomon, R. L., and Corbit, J. D. (1973). An opponent-process theory of motivation: I. Temporal dynamics of affect. *Psychological Review, 81,* 119–145.

Solomon, R. L., and Wynne, L. C. (1954). Traumatic avoidance learning: The principles of anxiety conservation and partial irreversibility. *Psychological Review, 61,* 353–385.

Spence, K. W. (1944). The nature of theory construction in contemporary psychology. *Psychological Review, 51,* 47–68.

Staddon, J. E. R. (1993). *Behaviorism: Mind, mechanism and society.* London: Duckworth.

Stevens, S. S. (1939). Psychology and the science of science. *Psychological Bulletin, 36,* 221–263.

Stevenson, H. W., Iscoe, I., and McConnell, C. A. (1955). A developmental study of transposition. *Journal of Experimental Psychology, 49,* 278–280.

Strang, J. P. (1989). Gastrointestinal disorders. In S. Cheren (ed.), *Psychosomatic medicine: Theory, physiology, and practice,* Vol. 2. Madison. Conn.: International Universities Press.

Thorndike, E. L. (1911. *Animal intelligence: Experimental studies.* New York: Macmillan.

Tolman, E. C. (1922). A new formula for behaviorism. *Psychological Review, 29,* 44–53.

Tolman, E. C. (1925). Purpose and cognition: The determiners of animal learning. *Psychological Review, 32,* 285–297.

Tolman, E. C. (1936). Operational behaviorism and current trends in psychology. *Proceedings of the 25th anniversary of the inauguration of graduate studies in psychology.* Los Angeles: University of Southern California Press.

Tolman, E. C. (1938). The determiners of behavior at a choice point. *Psychological Review, 45,* 1–41.

Tolman, E. C. (1951). *Collected papers in psychology.* Berkeley and Los Angeles: University of California Press.

Tulving, E., and Thompson, D. M. (1973). Encoding specificity and retrieval processes in episodic memory. *Psychological Review, 80,* 352–373.

Watson, J. B. (1913). Psychology as the behaviorist views it. *Psychological Review, 20,* 158–177.

Watson, J. B. (1925). *Behaviorism.* New York: Norton.

Weingartner, H., Aderfis, W., Eich, J. E., and Murphy, D. L. (1976). Encoding imagery specificity in alcohol state-dependent learning. *Journal of Experimental Psychology: Human Learning and Memory, 2,* 83–87.

Weiss, J. M. (1970). Somatic effects of predictable and unpredictable shock. *Psychosomatic Medicine, 32,* 397–408.

Werner, H. (1957). *Comparative psychology of mental development* (rev. ed.). New York: International Universities Press.

Wertheimer, M. (1912). Experimentelle Studien Uber das Sehen von Bewegung. *Zeitschrift fur Psychologie, 61,* 161–265.

Wolfe, J. B. (1936). Effectiveness of token-rewards for chimpanzees. *Comparative Psychology Monographs, 12,* no. 60.

Woodworth, R. L. (1919). Examination of emotional fitness for warfare. *Psychological Bulletin, 16,* 599–560.

Yerkes, R. M, and Dodson, J. D. (1908). The relation of strength of stimulus to rapidity of habit-formation. *Journal of Comparative Neurology and Psychology, 18,* 459–482.

Zacks, R. T., and Hasher, L. (1994). Directed ignoring: Inhibitory regulation of working memory. In D. Dagenbach and T. H. Carr (eds.), *Inhibitory mechanisms in attention, memory and language.* New York: Academic Press.

Zuckerman, M. (1991). *Psychobiology of personality.* New York: Cambridge University Press.

Index